FINDING THEIR OWN VOICES

Maine Women at the Millennium:
Their Stories

FINDING THEIR OWN VOICES
Maine Women at the Millennium:
Their Stories

Text and Photographs by
JAMES ANDREW MITCHELL

DOWN EAST BOOKS
CAMDEN, MAINE

ISBN 0-89272-587-7

Printed at Versa Press, East Peoria, Illinois

5   4   3   2   1

Cover and text design
by Chris McLarty, Silverline Studio, Camden, Maine

Down East Books
Camden, Maine
Book Orders: 1-800-685-7962
www.downeastbooks.com

Library of Congress Control Number: 2002109963

To my granddaughters, Elise and Hannah,
who are beginning to find their own voices.

CONTENTS

Introduction   ix

Foreword by Lyn Mikel Brown   xiii

Acknowledgements   xvii

Profiles

Agriculture and Fishing
   Linda Greenlaw   1
   Nanney Kennedy   7
   Betty Ann Listowich   11

Art
   Kate Barnes   15
   Mary Anne Driscoll   19
   Rosalind Morgan   23
   Marguerite Robichaux   27

Business
   Janet Harvie   31
   Kathy Ouellette   35

Civil Rights
   Kathryn McInnis-Misenor   39
   Penny Plourde   43

Independent, Miscellaneous Occupations
   Muriel Curtis   47
   Anneliese Francis   51

Nonprofit Organizations
   Karin Anderson   55
   Cate Cronin   59
   Karen Stimpson   63
   Sheila Tasker   69

Politics

    Lynn Bromley   **73**

    Brenda Commander   **79**

    Donna Loring   **83**

    Chellie Pingree   **87**

Service Professions

Law

    Janet C. McCaa   **93**

Medicine

    Yueer Ren   **97**

    Diane H. Schetky   **101**

    Joan Yeaton   **107**

Religion

    Susan Stonestreet   **113**

    Linda Thompson   **117**

Science

    Linda Alverson   **123**

    Ann Gibbs   **127**

Teaching

    Riva Berleant   **131**

    Melissa Hatch   **137**

    Sarah Hudson   **141**

List of Profiles

    by primary areas of involvement   **143**

INTRODUCTION

I have always done everything that Fred Astaire did,
except that I did it in high heels and going backward.
—Ginger Rogers, 1911–1995

W hy this book? That I grew up with and have known several
strong women is insufficient. I have seen women be too timid
to state what is truly on their mind, withhold their views to
keep the peace, or feel that their advice would not be heeded even if
advanced. Those reasons too are not enough.

It wasn't until I came across a certain quote by Gloria Steinem that
I fully understood what prompted this book. It helped explain an egre-
gious sexist put-down of my wife, Lolly. In a 1972 issue of *MS* magazine,
Steinem wrote: "Any woman who chooses to become a full human being
must be prepared to take on the armies of the status quo, who will try to
turn her into something of a dirty joke; that is their first and primary
weapon." Steinem's words described perfectly my wife's put-down, in the
face of which she and ten other professional women remained silent.

The situation that got my attention was Lolly's attempt to offer a
dissenting opinion at a board meeting. The head of the board, her
Harvard Business School instructor many years back, agreed to hear her
opinion, then announced that he had tried to look up her grades but
couldn't find them. "I guess I didn't keep the ladies' grades. I only kept
the men's. But I remember telling the ladies not to be afraid to challenge
the status quo. Well, so much for that advice!" Then, after laughing
uproariously at his "joke," he turned to my wife and asked if there was
anything more she wanted to say.

Her battle wasn't mine to fight, but could I do anything that might
bolster the self-assurance of today's young women to deal with such an
attack? I began thinking of the strong women I had known. The most

memorable older woman in my life was my grandmother. As a girl, she loved to ride horseback but refused to ride sidesaddle, which was the custom in the late 1800s. She also loved to ride alone in the Pennsylvania woods. So her father gave her a .32-caliber revolver and taught her how to use it. When she tired of waiting for her shy suitor to ask for her hand in marriage, she said to him sweetly one day, "I hope our children will be very happy." They married and had five children before her husband died young, at forty-five. She raised the children herself. Although she was not formally educated (girls back then received tutoring), she was extremely well read and could recite long passages of poetry from memory. It was a privilege to be with her, obey her, learn from her, and have her join in our activities, even mountain climbing until she was well into her seventies. Unconventional to the end, she requested that her ashes be scattered on her favorite trail and that no plaque ever be erected in her honor.

Another strong woman I knew was Susan Lewis, just under six feet tall and weighing close to two hundred pounds. She was a registered nurse with four older, bigger brothers who were protective of her. Because of them, she had few dates and despaired of ever having a social life in her home environment. In the mid-1950s she signed on as a missionary nurse in Fort Yukon, Alaska, on the Arctic Circle, where the sun doesn't rise in winter. Her summer beat was the settlements, mining camps, and logging operations along seven hundred miles of the Yukon River, which she traversed in a johnboat with only a native guide for company. She'd set up her traveling clinic at each stop and tend to wounds, broken limbs, and an occasional serious operation, which she carried out while in radio contact with the lone doctor at the home clinic. When I saw her several years later, she never mentioned fear, just the job that had to be done. She had numerous suitors, although she chose none of them.

I knew other women who were not all they could have been. A budding artist wouldn't show her work for many years because she felt it wasn't good enough. A woman I grew up with had been brainwashed into believing that women were second-class citizens. Another friend, afraid she wouldn't be advanced because of her gender, didn't try to get a better job. All of these—the successes, the lack of self-confidence, the put-downs—are my inspiration for this book.

I have known for a long time that women tell their stories to other women and that these stories become every woman's story. I decided to gather together a number of stories that strong, independent women tell about themselves and their achievements in order to form a collective message. This message is to all women that they can do anything they set out to do. I wanted to include stories of women who overcame tremendous difficulties. I wanted to present the choices women have to make to balance work and other elements of their lives. I decided to find a group of role models—women who have been successful in nontraditional careers—so women reading about other women could say, "Hey, I could do that." Who knows, perhaps such stories could help men as well by leveling the field between women and men and helping eradicate some of the patriarchal hierarchy, which is slowly being nudged aside but still exists.

Of the many women who told me their stories and dreams, thirty-two are profiled here. This book belongs largely to these women. Although more than half of them came here from other parts of the country, the scope of this book is limited to women now working and living in Maine. This is because I live here and because something about this state seems to promote independent thinking. Not only was Margaret Chase Smith the first woman senator in the country, the state now has two women senators, an Independent governor, and a sizeable and growing number of women legislators.

I decided early to largely exclude women who had risen already to high positions or who were highly visible. I wanted women who could be accessible role models. The women I chose are married, with and without children, or are single, divorced, partnered, or single moms. Some are "from away"; some are true Mainers. They live in all parts of the state. Although most are Anglo-Saxon, there are representatives of other ethnic groups, including Native Americans, African Americans, Asian Americans, and Jews. They participate or have been involved in well over seventy different occupations, most of which were not open to women until the last few decades.

Although their stories are different, they all celebrate the remarkable resilience of the human spirit. What these women have in common is intelligence, passion, and enthusiasm; a belief in their own abilities; and a go-to place for spiritual help or recharging their batteries. They have developed a sure sense of who they are, or are working hard to achieve it. Without exception they are highly moral, in the sense that they remain true to their own selves, although a number live unconventional lives.

Presenting such a diverse group of women has been a challenge. How to best arrange their stories so that the reader can easily refer to those dealing with their own interest? An alphabetical listing is of little help; sorting them by some motivational distinction leads to making subjective judgments. The one chosen is listing them by their primary area of current involvement—current because many of these women have done numerous things in their lives.

Were these women influenced by common factors? No. Their backgrounds, whether they had strong role models or weak ones, or whether they had to fight for independence, are as diverse as the individuals themselves. Some, but far from all, did have a parent or grandparent who encouraged them to be all they could be. But what seems to count most is that almost all have an inborn "feisty spirit"—an attitude that carves out its own sphere of independence regardless of what messages are being received. In a few, such a spirit developed because of a particular event; in some others, it grew or formed in response to being overcontrolled by a parent, but in many it appears to be an inborn belief in themselves that appeared very early

Working on this book has proven to be one of the most exciting and rewarding experiences of my life, as well as a tremendous learning opportunity. I have had the rare chance to meet and get to know many remarkable women. They have shared stories about personal areas of their lives. They have shown me that women can do anything they set out to do, and in some areas are better able than men to handle a job. I refer here to their strengths in verbal communication, their ability to handle several tasks at the same time, and their desire for consensus in achieving a goal. Additionally, women appear to have a greater need for community: They are the keepers of our rituals, the guardians of our young.

After reading these profiles, it is not a big leap to conclude that if women receive greater encouragement to become all they can be, they can excel in any occupation for which they develop a passion. To quote one of these extraordinary women: "The only limits on a young woman's options and choices are the limits she puts on herself." That is the message of this book.

Camden, Maine

FOREWORD

By Lyn Mikel Brown

Associate Professor of Women's Studies, Education, and Human Development at Colby College

My mother's mother was one of seven sisters; her grandmother was one of five. There were a few brothers scattered here and there, but women defined the family spirit. My mother was an only daughter, tied by a single resolute thread to a formidable matriarchy. The daughters of Roix were ancestors of Huguenots who escaped to New Brunswick, Canada and Washington County, Maine from France. Renegades all of them. Feisty and tireless women, they passed on a mixture of radical independence, stubbornness, and a particularly intense flavor of love and responsibility. My six great-aunts helped raise my mother—doted on her, challenged her, fought with her. They were everything to me as a child—old women, other mothers, safe havens, teachers, muses. They were women of the Earth. One great-aunt taught me to cook my first pie and to crochet, another to walk in the woods and find spruce gum to chew, another to fish from the bridge beside the dam, another to cherish long canoe rides to deserted beaches and once there to find sea glass and jasper. They were, above all, women of spirit, old souls who rejoiced in one another. Fearless and buoyant, they were unafraid of what cruelties the world might hand them. They were funny, irreverent, and loud, and they loved with an intensity that oozed from their pores and filled the cracks of their old houses with warmth in winter. My mother is like them in so many ways. We were poor when I was young. My mother cared for four children and an ill mother-in-law while my father left, for a week at a time, to work on the railroad. She sewed new clothes, she mended old ones; she put wigs on old dolls, dressed them up, and put them under the Christmas tree. She saved everything—paper, string, boxes, bits of material. Nothing wasted. And she loved us—loves us still—like a mother bear, with the force and fullness she inherited from a maternal lineage as old as the Maine hills.

I carry these women with me. They ground me. They are the ancestors I cry out to in moments of despair, the muses I call on when my creative juices have run dry and I feel discouraged and hopeless. Forget about it, they would cackle. Let's take a walk in the woods, look at the robin and her chicks on the highest branch, paint this dresser mint green, have some soup. What do you care what they think?

I love this book because it is filled with the voices of those women who taught me the most about how to live. The advice and wisdom I thought defined my family alone weave through the pages, passed down in loving memory. Other women have learned the same lessons, I see. Other women from a great variety of backgrounds and experiences were loved and challenged in ways that brought their lives to creative fruition. What do they care what others think? You are your passion, they tell us. Love hard. Push your own limits. Make the world a more beautiful place. This is wisdom that comes from the school of hard knocks, that says even if you don't have a pot to piss in or a window to throw it out of, you have choices and your world turns on them. This book is a promise to generations of Maine girls that there are countless pathways to fulfillment, to economic security, to self-respect, and to pleasure in life, pathways limited only by our own creativity and our willingness to work hard and believe in ourselves.

In Maine we know about hard work, of course; it's a knowledge that runs through our veins. Most of us have had to piece life together at some point or another; we've had to fix our own toilets, clean our own houses, make a Christmas turkey last into February. The women in our pasts too often nurtured their passions in the fractured spaces between caring for others, in moments bent over the ironing board, between loads of laundry. The women in this book pay homage to such resolve and creativity, grabbing hold of what once was so elusive to all but a chosen few. They show us that passion nurtured, fed on the light and fresh air of devotion, determination, and some measure of support from somewhere or someone, turns into a meaningful and chosen life. Such a life has many names, many identities; it is not trapped in the monochromatic, but is a prism, a dizzying array of colors that shocks us with its patterned brilliance. We can have this kind of life, these women tell us. We can have it whether or not we have money or a lot of education, although clearly these gifts make the path smoother. We can have it even if someone has tried to beat the living tar out of us or has told us over and over again how worthless we are. We can create a life that is joyous and worth living, that is ours alone.

My great grandmother and her sisters, my grandmother and her sisters, would love this book. They would sit at their kitchen tables and ooh and aah over these brave, wild, fearless women and they would count themselves among them. I see this book not only as a gift to our daughters, but a wonderful testimony to the many invisible and unnamed Maine women who have come before.

ACKNOWLEDGEMENTS

This book would not have happened had it not been for the input and encouragement of many people—from the man whose egregiously sexist put down of my wife, Lolly, got me started, to Gloria Steinem's writings, which helped me understand what Lolly had been through, to all the wonderful, fearless women who told me their stories and encouraged me to finish this book. Their hope, and mine, is that it will provide young women with some road maps to help them on their way to whatever they might achieve—which can be anything they set their hearts on.

Most particularly, though, I need to single out a few of those women who have truly made a difference in helping this work along, from contributing names and providing initial contacts to maintaining a keen interest in the book's progress, and who have helped in editing to make the language sing:

Karin Anderson, of the Maine Women's Fund, for her support of the project from the beginning, for providing names of women to include, and for providing a number of contacts.

Lynn Bromley and **Penny Plourde** in particular for suggesting some remarkable women to include in addition to providing their own stories of survival, growth, and success.

The other strong and independent women in this book who have refused to take "no" for an answer and have persevered in creating lives for themselves that are way out of the ordinary.

Lyn Mikel Brown, Associate Professor of Women's Studies, Education, and Human Development at Colby College, whose forward to to this book celebrates the lives of a number of her female ancestors together with her comments on the importance of this work.

Barbara Feller-Roth who has provided her editing expertise and other guidance to make this book hold together and present these many women as full, living, and loving human beings.

And **Lolly Mitchell**, my wife, who has suffered through the creation of this work, endured my absences, and always provided sound advice along with her skill as an editor.

Classic overachiever and risk taker

LINDA GREENLAW

Isle au Haut, Maine   Born 1960
Swordfishing boat captain, lobster fisherman, author

For many living on the coast of Maine, inshore fishing is a way of life and a time-honored profession. This is particularly true of island communities with no other way to make a living. It is arduous work, whether fishing for lobsters, clamming, trawling for scallops or shrimp, or engaging in the newer industry of salmon farming. It is also not without risk; there is no guaranteed income and, as with all work in New England waters, it involves dealing with fog and bad weather. There are also occasional accidents, sometimes resulting in death. At the same time it means independence, where hard work can produce its own rewards, and there is a rhythm and a feeling of satisfaction in this way of life.

There is another not so visible fishing industry—offshore fishing, where big boats go out to the banks to long-line for swordfish. With modern equipment and refrigeration, these boats stay out for thirty days or more at a stretch. If they're lucky, they may return with 50,000 pounds of fish. With a good catch, the rewards in crew shares can be significant. But the reverse can also be true, because all the costs of operating the boats are taken out first. The risks are proportionally greater than for inshore fishing. So are the hardships of being at sea continuously for thirty days at a time—usually with quick turnarounds during the season. It is a lifestyle that makes developing and maintaining a shoreside social life difficult if not impossible. But the excitement of catching fish is a potent force for some.

It is this offshore fishing that attracted Linda Greenlaw after she graduated from Colby College. Even during college, she shipped out on

1

swordfishing boats during summers to help defray her college costs. It was a natural outgrowth of growing up in a family with its roots on Isle au Haut. Though her father worked at Bath Iron Works and she went to school in Topsham, summers were always spent on the island, where fishing was never far from anyone's mind. Linda followed this path for seventeen years. She went from being part of the crew to becoming captain of the *Gloria Dawn*, a long-line swordfishing boat with a crew of five based in Portland. This was her first command, which she had for three seasons.

After some time and several other boats, Linda took command of the *Hannah Boden*, another long-liner based in Gloucester, Massachusetts. It was here that she developed the reputation of being one of the best swordfishing captains on the entire East Coast. She was also the only woman captain. The sister ship to the *Hannah Boden* was the *Andrea Gail*, the boat and crew whose loss was vividly described by Sebastian Junger in his book *The Perfect Storm*, and later in the movie of the same name.

How did Linda develop the desire and confidence to become such an outstanding fishing boat captain? Two stories help illuminate how she was encouraged at a tender age to become who she is. The first occurred when she was seven, during a family summer picnic on an island adjacent to Isle au Haut. Told by one of the adults that the boys should go off and cut marshmallow sticks and the girls should go find driftwood for the fire, Linda ran off with the boys because, as she says, "I had my own jackknife." Forced to return to go with the girls, she sat down and cried. When her mother asked Linda what was wrong, she replied, "Do I have to be a girl?" Her mother replied, "No, you can be whatever you want to be." Linda says, "Suddenly, the whole world was right for me. So I ran off to be with the boys."

The second event happened while Linda was in high school in Topsham. She was an excellent student and at the top of her class—not, she says, "because I had any particular God-given abilities, but because I was taught to work hard and had always done so." One day, a teacher whom she adored referred to her as the "classic overachiever." Linda says, "I was deeply insulted, because it meant I was just average but worked hard. That hurt because I thought I was pretty brilliant at that point in my life! But ... now I'm proud of being an overachiever—I can get very focused on one thing—I can work hard and get good at whatever I want to do."

What Linda always wanted to do was go fishing. She makes a claim that few can equal: "I have never worked for a wage. It has always been for a crew share or for selling the fish that I've caught." Linda bristles somewhat over gender distinctions and language. For her there is no reason why she shouldn't be the captain of a fishing boat. She dislikes being termed a "fisherwoman." She doesn't understand why some men as well as other women were surprised that she was a captain or that any of the crew would have problems with her being in command. She says she has never had the slightest difficulty with her crews over her gender. She didn't even seem to mind that they sometimes referred to her as "mother." To Linda it was a job—a job that she did well, from handling the many problems in getting a boat to sea without forgetting something that would be sorely missed, to maintaining it well, keeping the crew focused and fed, watching the weather, and locating fish. It is all of these things, which Linda seemed to do exceptionally well, that led to her reputation as an outstanding captain.

But at the age of thirty-six—seventeen years after starting—Linda stopped swordfishing. "I was pretty much at the top of my game. There was really no way for me to improve my lot in life workwise. I had the best boat on the eastern seaboard. I was doing very well ... but there was nowhere to go but down. The federal government had imposed a 30,000-pound trip limit, which meant there was no way for a good captain to distinguish himself, or herself. It takes the element of competition right out of it.

Also ... my maternal instincts were beginning to really kick in. I wanted a boyfriend. There's something about, 'Thanks for dinner. See you in thirty days.' You don't get many second dates. In fact it's tough to maintain any kind of relationship at all ... I got to an age where I wanted—and I still very much want—to have children. So I had this idea that I would like to get home ... My folks were getting older; my nieces and nephews seemed to have grown up while I wasn't looking."

Coming home for Linda didn't mean she would stop fishing, just that she would change to lobstering. She bought a boat, named it the *Maddie Belle* after her grandmother, and started fishing out of Isle au Haut. Her father, who had retired by this time to the island, often sailed with her as sternman. More recently she has built herself a home on the island.

Not long after Linda returned to the island, her plans were interrupted. With the publication of Junger's book *The Perfect Storm*, and the subsequent interest in turning it into a movie, Linda was asked to write her own book on the subject, and was given a sizable advance. Out of this effort came *The Hungry Ocean*, a first-rate account of the technical as well as the human side of what it means to captain a swordfishing boat. It is told with humor, honesty, and compassion. Even Sebastian Junger calls it "the best book, period, that I've ever read on fishing." Talking about her chance to write this book, Linda alludes to another prime driving force within her. "I think that 'opportunity' is the most important word in the English language. Obviously, I've had some good opportunities, but I like the phrase 'opportunity knocks.' Opportunity knocks, but it doesn't let itself in. You have to answer the door. I think that's where the hard work comes in for people like me."

Linda's dream is still to have a family. Part of this comes from her own growing up. "My parents loved each other, and there was no 'divide and conquer'; they were a team. I thought my father was Superman. I would be thrilled to meet a man that I could say the same things about to my children as my mother said to me about my father." In the meantime, with the publication of her first book, Linda has been asked to write a second—about the transition from offshore fishing to a new life.

Fishing, yes, but also having a home base and roots back on her island. She would be willing to live anywhere, but she could never give up Isle au Haut. It is home to her as it is to her brother and sister, both of whom live elsewhere but come home when they can.

Portland, Maine

*There's always one moment
in childhood when the door
opens and lets the future in.*

— Graham Greene

Preserving Maine's agricultural heritage in wool growing

NANNEY KENNEDY

Washington, Maine   Born 1960
Sheep farmer, entrepreneur, mentor to young girls

This handsome, strong-boned, high-energy woman single-handedly runs a sheep farm, is working to upgrade wool growing in the state, and runs a blanket business and hand-dyeing business. She is also rebuilding her house and barn, which were destroyed by fire. From temporary quarters over her garage, where she lives with her ten- and thirteen-year-old sons, Nanney looks out over her eighty acres of rolling pastureland and talks about her life.

"My husband is no longer in the picture. My current male friend isn't much help either. It was his dog that was responsible for killing over twenty of my sheep last winter, and he still hasn't apologized." Despite all this, she appears to be coping without undo worry with what life throws at her.

"I was definitely raised with the concept that there was nothing I couldn't do if I set my mind to it," says Nanney. Her godmother, a crack shot, was part of Wild Bill Hickok's show and was hired by the army during both world wars to teach soldiers how to shoot. Her grandparents started Camp Kieve in Nobleboro, which her grandmother kept running, after her grandfather became involved with another woman, hoping that it would continue for her sons. Nanney was sent away from home for coed camp, because Kieve was for boys only. Nanney's father and mother helped found the Pingree School north of Boston and also managed the camp.

Nanney was defiant early on. If her father said not to do something, it was what she immediately set out to do. She says now that she and her father are a lot alike, although she describes him as "an egomaniac." He encouraged her to think for herself, yet his public challenges to her authority in meetings produce sparks, which often result in her leaving in tears and other members trying to comfort her. She says that she sometimes went to her mother and asked, "Why the hell was I born to this man?"

At Bowdoin College Nanney became enamored of the William Morris tradition of handcrafts in the commercial marketplace. Her interest in rural sociology with the need for community and its values and work ethic were paired with a desire to have a positive impact on society. After graduation she decided to start a fiber business, but the sheep whose wool was desirable for spinning and weaving were no longer being raised in Maine. So she worked her way to New Zealand on a boat to learn the wool business firsthand in an economy totally dependent on sheep. There she worked for a farmer and his wife to learn what she needed to know to start her own business.

Returning to Maine, Nanney bought her farm with money she had saved beginning when she started babysitting at age twelve. She developed a flock whose wool could be used in fine blankets and sweaters. Because Maine's wool-processing plants were no longer in business, Nanney found and still uses mills in the Canadian Maritimes to perform all the necessary operations: washing, scouring, carding, blending colors, spinning, and weaving. When her house burned and she was in danger of losing everything, fortune stepped in through the distribution of her godmother's estate, from which she received enough to keep going.

In New Zealand, Nanney had learned about the importance of feed as well as breed type on wool quality. Good feed can make the difference between low-quality wool selling for ten cents a pound and top-quality wool that sells for $1.25 a pound. So Nanney set out to offer high prices to growers around Maine for good wool grades and to help the industry develop by offering the growers quality breeding stock. In addition, she works with growers on a cooperative basis in the blanket business, so the farmers receive a many-fold increase on their wool price. She has also developed a summer hand-dyeing business using a seawater–solar process that is suited to Maine.

Will Nanney succeed in all her endeavors? Although it means living close to the bone, it won't be for lack of hard work and trying. Fortunately, Nanney's half-time work for Camp Kieve, both as a board member and on the staff, helps support her family. On the few occasions when she is not working, Nanney says she finds great spiritual support through her association with a group of women that trains working dogs for sheep farming.

Nanney is involved in a science camp for girls in the fifth to seventh grades at Camp Kieve. In addition, she acts as a mentor to local girls, helping them to raise their expectations of what they can achieve. She has given up for now trying to teach suburban girls "who come with their daddy's credit cards wanting to be paid, but also wanting time off so they can go to shows and buy their fancy clothes." She says she does not "feel valued by that process."

Washington, Maine

Built her business where she loves to be

BETTY ANN LISTOWICH

Kingfield, Maine   Born 1959

Founder of commercial landscape contracting business

Hydroseeding vast areas, planting trees as windbreaks, and establishing erosion-control plantings along miles of roadside, in large housing developments, on golf courses. This is what Betty Ann Listowich's landscape construction firm, Norpine Landscaping, does. She loves her work and the life it provides.

Betty Ann's vision for combining a way to make a living with loving where she lives began shortly after college, when she started working for the Sugarloaf ski patrol—only the fourth woman to have that position. Several years later after finding out that the mountain was putting in a golf course and the state was putting in sewer beds, she decided that a landscaping business was a perfect way to work summers and ski winters. She and her future husband Jim, who had moved to nearby Kingfield, started the landscaping business in 1984. She became a finish worker on the golf course, and Jim seeded the sewer beds. Another four years and they expanded the business to service state road contracts, investing in all the necessary specialized equipment, such as hydroseeders and tree planters in addition to plows, harrows, power rakes, and so on.

Betty Ann has not only built a successful business but combined it with living where she loves to be so she can ski in the winter as well as spend most of her life out-of-doors the remainder of the year. "Everything I've done, I've done because I like doing it. I love working with plants, I love working outdoors ... I'm in heaven being outside. I love it as the weather changes around me—the sights, sounds, and smells of nature."

Now with two small children, life has changed somewhat for her. She no longer works with the ski patrol. The childrens' demands mean balancing her needs with theirs—changing her focus, but in ways that she feels are healthy in each season.

Half French-Canadian, part Irish, and part Cherokee, Betty Ann spent her childhood in South Freeport, mostly in the same house. Her mother was especially nurturing and wanted the family to spend a lot of time together. They traveled to Saddleback Mountain and skied together most winter weekends. She revered her grandfather—her mother's father—a self-made man who was kind, gentle, and strong—a true patriarch of a large French family. Her father encouraged her to do and be anything she wanted, as long as she tried to be the best she could be at whatever she chose. She was headstrong by the time she was twelve, when her mother died. Through her father's remarriage, Betty Ann and her two older sisters gained a younger brother and sister.

She attended local schools, then the University of Maine at Orono. She wanted to become an architect, but family finances precluded her going to a college where that was an option, so she majored in political science and history. She met Jim in college.

Several years after starting the landscaping business they bought a farm in Kingfield where they planted their fields with the types of trees and shrubs they hoped to use in their contracts or sell to other landscapers. Betty Ann studied every book she could find to learn the technical side of the business. She studied to get the license allowing her to drive larger trucks. The curiosity and learning never stopped. By investing wisely and living simply, they now own the business free and clear, including the farm and house they live in with their two school-aged children.

Betty Ann is instantly likeable. She has a lot of energy and seems to be in constant motion. She is like the "Energizer Bunny." She is also organized. There's no question that she runs the business. Yet in meetings, Jim, who is six-foot-six (Betty Ann is five-five), tells clients who look to him that they should talk to her. And they do. At the same time, it is the design work and talking with clients about plants that gives her the most satisfaction.

Betty Ann and Jim love to get out on the mountain and ski in the backcountry. She has taken her own advice: "Find a way to enjoy your life and live it, [whether it] means organizing or administering or making a landscape look perfect and orderly … or getting out and exercising.

Do whatever it takes to make yourself happy. If you like to work and you like what you do, and you like bouncing out of bed in the morning and going to your job, you'll do really well at it, and the money will come."

Kingfield, Maine

Celebrating our connection to nature

KATE BARNES

Appleton Ridge, Maine   Born 1932
Maine's first poet laureate

Listening to Kate talk about her life or read her poetry is like being transported to an earlier, gentler century: the buckboard on the lane, the smell of fresh cut hay, the peace and quiet of evening. This is Maine as it was and still is when you find your way inland from the coast. This is Appleton Ridge, where Kate makes her home alone near where she grew up. It is her sanctuary now. It is where she came to write poetry again after her children were grown and her marriage was over. It is where she came to share her mother's last days.

Kate returned to Maine after years of living in the San Gabriel Mountains of California. She came back more than anything because it was her natural place. "Maine is just one of the least ruined places. We are living in a world that has got to turn itself about. We are living in a world that we are ruining so fast." She quotes from one of her father's letters: "What I stand for is . . . the return to a poetic relation to nature. Humankind is out of relation to its background, and its blood has grown spiritually and psychically thin. When humankind is in poetic relation to its background, it achieves a religious sense of life and it is this sense which makes us human. Without a poetic relation to nature and to a sense of our own destiny, we are no better than a woodchuck, perhaps not as good."

Despite her belief that we are perishing from our lack of connection to nature, Kate believes there is room for hope. Although she is upset with what she sees happening in the world, she sees bright spots: People are beginning to think seriously about ecology and are starting to make changes in the way they live.

Kate's poetry describes the rural countryside of Maine and earned her the honor of becoming Maine's first poet laureate. But her poetry is about more than that; it is about our humanity and the importance of our relationship to nature in all its guises. It celebrates our strengths, our longings, our loneliness, and our sexuality. It is the poetry of a woman who sees and feels much and can express herself with clarity.

One of Kate's poems captures much of this in just four lines:

> *While the horses strain at the harrow in a darkening field,*
>   *I pour red wine over lentils in an iron kettle.*
> *The full moon rising beyond the farm graveyard is as round as a well,*
>   *and the cold autumn wind has the taste of distant water.*

As a child Kate spent her winters in Massachusetts and summers with her parents at their farm in Nobleboro. It was there that her father, Henry Beston, wrote *The Outermost House,* a classic that is still in print, and *Northern Farm,* about life on the farm and the changing of the seasons. Her mother, Elizabeth Coatsworth, wrote numerous poems and children's books. Kate's love of writing, particularly poetry, arose naturally out of these strong links to her parents and to the farm where, as she says, "We didn't actually raise anything. The hay was cut and we had a nice big garden, but it was a farm in the sense of raising something—it raised words ..."

Kate's mother was a strong role model who could concentrate on her writing, yet drop it in an instant to address some interruption. She was loving and diplomatic, could tend to her husband's needs, then give a little shake and return in an instant to pick up her train of thought. Kate remembers her having a complete life and doing everything. She was an early feminist, a suffragette in the days when women were first allowed to vote. Her mother's ability and independent streak earned her bitter rebukes from her father, who would say, "American women, American women," which was his way of swearing at her for not doing whatever it was that he wanted. Part of his exasperation was because, after his classic, *The Outermost House,* was published, he had difficulty concentrating on his writing and spent much time setting up little studios around the farm for privacy. Kate says she was never quite comfortable with her father, whom she describes as awe inspiring and quick tempered. But his words did "get into her," as she says, and may have contributed as much to her becoming a poet as any other single influence.

Following college, Kate fell in love with a charismatic teacher, married him, and moved to California, where he taught English at Pomona

College. The marriage soon soured when he began drinking heavily. She would beg him to stay home at least some evenings instead of frequenting the Mexican bars. Later, when tenure kept eluding him at college, the brandy bottle would go into his briefcase as he left in the morning. She says she might have left him except for their four children and the fact that she, like many women of her generation, had no marketable skills.

In a long poem she later wrote about her life, she describes the tile floor where her head is lying and being banged about. Her husband, in a drunken rage, is punching her face and shouting, "Be more submissive, damn it! Be more submissive!" She lies as still as possible, trying not to struggle, sobbing only to try to win some small degree of sympathy. She thinks, but I am utterly submissive, then realizes that he sees something in her that she has never given up completely—a stubbornness, an assumption that she still exists. His behavior changed after Kate made it plain that she would leave if it ever happened again. He never hit her again. Finally, with her children grown, Kate was able to make the break and get a divorce. These words are from her poem during a last meeting where she desperately hoped for one final, kind word from him:

> Could that be true?
> Of course not! Has he ever forgiven anyone
> who turned him down? He is really
> more bitter than ever. He'd like to make a last
> gesture, all right, he'd like to belt her one—

Returning to Maine, Kate bought her farm on Appleton Ridge, not far from where she summered in Nobleboro as a child, and began to write poetry after a hiatus of twenty-five years. Some of her new work was published in a volume entitled *Where the Deer Were*, an edition of which is illustrated by Mary Azarian's woodblock prints. Other work has appeared in *Harper's*, *The New Yorker*, *The Village Voice*, *New England Review*, and *Harvard Review*.

Kate says of her poems, "If you read them, you know me." She is sensitive. She recalls the bad times but is not bitter. She is at once wise and thoughtful as she celebrates our humanity and the connection of all things to nature.

Appleton, Maine

Enthusiastic, inquisitive, free thinker

MARY ANNE DRISCOLL

Belfast, Maine   Born 1950

Jazz musician, composer, teacher, bandleader, mother

" I believe that love, understanding, and learning are all closely inter-
woven in life and somehow I've seen this from the time I was
young ... You learn to accept that life isn't fair, it's not about being
fair. It's that we're alive, with an opportunity to discover ... I have a very
strong sense that ... it's not what I can get out of life, it's what I can give
to life."

Humor, jazz, singing, and dancing with her sister filled the house
from the time Mary Anne was a girl in California's Bay Area. So did two
older siblings and a younger brother. So did Uncle Charley, her father's
brother, who was a fairly constant presence playing the jazz trumpet,
knowing the words to all the songs, and teaching Mary Anne about love
and reincarnation—he didn't even want to kill a fly. Catholic school
exposed Mary Anne to classical music; she sang in the choir from an
early age. Her father left when she was six. Her older brother, who was
brilliant, introduced Mary Anne to Mozart and physics. One of the nuns
at school gave Mary Anne an excellent education in music. She was a top
student in religion at school until she was thrown out of class for challenging accepted Catholic dogma. She was transferred to a one-on-one
philosophy course where her questions would not visibly upset her teachers. When her father, whom she loved greatly, was diagnosed with termi-
nal cancer, he came back to make peace with his family. He talked to her
and her brother about nonviolence and Thoreau's beliefs. He died a few
months after her brother was killed in the Vietnam War.

Realizing early that the truth can be elusive, and life isn't always
fair, Mary Anne questioned everything. She studied music in several

19

colleges in the Bay Area but pursued other subjects with a vengeance. While still in college, she fell in love with Paul Murphy, a percussionist, and they began to improvise together. She began composing her own music and performed avant-garde jazz with Paul in San Francisco, winning acclaim from jazz critics for their unique sound. In 1977 two great New York Jazz musicians, Cecil Taylor and Jimmy Lyons, invited them to New York—the jazz mecca—to play.

For Mary Anne, life in New York meant hard work as a waitress and a paralegal, while also composing, performing, and recording. The mother of two daughters, she describes their births as "the most ecstatic moments of my life." But her relationship with Paul came apart and he returned to San Francisco when the girls were still young. In 1990 Mary Anne moved to Maine. She taught piano in Belfast and Camden, then started a jazz quintet with four men, who insisted the group be named after her. She raised her daughters but never stopped composing, singing, and playing. She and her band were recently invited to Hungary to play. She says, "I'm not unhappy that I didn't get to be an artist because I had children. I'm an artist, and I'm raising my children. If it weren't for my children I couldn't do art. I got to become me and still be a mom."

This woman with such a bubbly and vital approach to life dispenses advice to her daughters based on her life experiences: "First discover what you can learn, what you can know … Develop your ability to understand things, then seek all the different areas where that occurs … A pattern will form that really draws your attention. Let yourself be drawn to that, rather than saying I have to become something … because it's almost impossible to do that without experience. You learn from the external world; the world can teach you what draws your interest, then that balance can lead in a satisfying way to a path to follow."

Belfast, Maine

*Guided by my heritage of a love
of beauty and a respect for strength—
in search of my mother's garden,
I found my own.*

— Alice Walker

A willingness to gamble

ROSALIND MORGAN

Linneus, Maine   Born 1958
Photographer, singer, business owner, weight lifter

" I learned only a couple of weeks ago in competition that I thought my body couldn't do diddly-squat in power lifting but I asked my body for close to the impossible and it responded, so I guess there is a belief in self—a willingness to gamble. If you're going to be in business for yourself, it's a gamble; if you're going into a relationship, that's a gamble. Sometimes you need to gamble; at other times you need to know that this is not a good day to gamble."

Within Maine, few stories are as worthy of attention as that of Rosalind's. For starters, she's an African-American living in the Houlton area of Aroostook County. In addition to developing an infrared aerial photography business to help pinpoint areas of cropland that are deficient in fertilizer, and singing with the Houlton chorus or performing solo at the local coffeehouse and in churches, she is a title-holding power lifter who competes on a national level in squat, bench press, and dead lift events. Her passion is nature-related photography; one of her several published photographs ran as a two-page spread in *Reader's Digest*. This interest led to her involvement in organizing group art shows in Aroostook County.

Although Rosalind has taken several gambles since coming to Aroostook County seventeen years ago, perhaps the biggest was deciding to move there in the first place. She and her partner bought 111 acres of land in Linneus, basically their own private nature preserve. How did Rosalind develop the sure sense of self to do these things?

Rosalind grew up in Washington, D.C., in middle-class circumstances. Being quite dark skinned, she was teased by her classmates and sometimes came home from school in tears. Luckily, she had a strong mother, who was a registered nurse, and an especially strong-minded grandmother, who taught her how to fight and insisted she never come home crying again. She didn't, although during her school years, black became beautiful, and the teasing stopped.

Music was Rosalind's primary interest in high school. She then enrolled at the University of Wisconsin in Milwaukee, majoring in music and music therapy, with her voice as her major instrument. In her junior year she realized she didn't want to deal with the bureaucratic requirements involved in music therapy, so she changed her major to outdoor education. Unfortunately the national economic and political climate was not right for becoming a forest ranger, and Rosalind dropped out of college in her senior year.

Though her mother and grandmother had been strong role models in helping Rosalind develop, it was her father she emulated after dropping out of college. A photographer for the U.S. Postal Service for many years, he had given Rosalind a Pentax camera and encouraged her interest in photography. While in college she started taking pictures, getting one or two published in the Milwaukee papers. Then she started photographing weddings—Polish weddings at that, which included not just the event itself but parties and dinners two and three days before, and dances afterward. That was hard on her grades. She says, "You can't pay me enough to do weddings now." But it was photography that led Rosalind to the New Jersey–New York area— that and someone she met teaching at a Girl Scout camp during college. Finding work in the city was difficult but, after improving her skills, her photographs began to be published.

Seeking to escape the increasingly urban character of New Jersey, Rosalind and her partner began looking for rural property in New England, eventually narrowing their search to Maine, then specifically the Houlton area, where they spotted a property with a geodesic dome house. They negotiated a deal, lined up jobs, went back to New Jersey, and prepared to move. Upon arriving in Maine in June 1983, they found that the jobs had dried up, so they cut broccoli and harvested potatoes to pay the mortgage. It was through these jobs that Rosalind learned that the University of Maine was looking into using infrared photography to spot stress in crops. She got in touch with the Maine Potato Board, found out what was needed, and started doing it on a trial basis in collaboration with a local flying service. Out of this, her niche business was born in 1985 and continues to grow.

Rosalind's photography led to her involvement with other Aroostook County artists, helping form the Houlton Center for the Arts and putting on an Aroostook Arts Gala. She had fun but it was not a huge success. With help from a grant from the Maine Arts Commission, Rosalind is working on a directory of artists for southern Aroostook County.

Health problems and a sense of being out of shape led to Rosalind's interest in weight lifting. At the age of forty, with encouragement from her coach, she entered the Maine State Championships—and won in her weight class. She was hooked. After more training, she entered the New England Championships, where she placed second. Knowing that knee replacement surgery would likely be necessary were she to stop lifting weights, she continues working at it.

This remarkable woman comes by her can-do attitude in part from her mother—who believes that people can do whatever they decide they want to do—but mainly from within herself. She knows who she is and is not afraid to take risks. Her advice is to be flexible. "If things don't work out one way, look for the alternatives. Learn to rely on yourself, but know when to reach out for help. Get the support you need, but know that you are capable of far more than you think."

Houlton, Maine

Preserving a beautifully observed world that's disappearing

MARGUERITE ROBICHAUX

Eustis, Maine   Born 1951
Visual artist of the natural world

" I think it's important to have a passion. Some are more defined than others, and some come to us later in life than they do for others. I happened to understand when I was very young that making visual art was what I really wanted to do, and I was fortunate to learn early that I was good at it. I had a sense of the visual, and I was dexterous enough to do it.

"I think encouraging and educating our passion is important. I've been able to follow mine, but not at the expense of someone else. Family and friends know they always come first. As much as I may want to lock myself in my studio, if friends need something, they come before my work. I believe in being kind to people, letting them be who they are. I believe in trying to do something in my life, however small it may be, to make the world a better place or a more beautifully observed place."

Marguerite Robichaux lives alone in a handsome house that she helped design and build. Overlooking a river and lake, it is part house, part studio, one space flowing into the next and filled with her art. The modern structure is in a remote area of western Maine yet appears completely comfortable in its surroundings. As does Marguerite. Although this house is new, she has lived in the area full-time for twenty years and had visited for several years prior to that.

Painting and drawing have been the focus of Marguerite's life since her childhood in Baton Rouge, Louisiana. "My mother gave me my first easel and smock and palette when I was about seven years old and encouraged me to paint from the time I was a little kid. While she would have preferred I do something else that would allow me to earn a living, when she realized that I was going to be an artist when I grew up, she did support me in it."

Marguerite and her mother, Gladys, were always close friends, and her mother was her primary role model. After she divorced Marguerite's father, Gladys went back to school to learn the tools to earn a living. She worked for the civil service (until retiring at the age of sixty-two) to provide Marguerite with whatever help she could. That included seeing that Marguerite was able to attend Louisiana State University, then Louisiana Tech, where she received her undergraduate degree, then back to Louisiana State for her master's degree in fine art. Along the way Marguerite married, then followed her husband to Houston, where he was finishing up work to become a physician's assistant. Marguerite did technical illustration to earn a living, then freelanced in the oil and gas industry or whatever else came along for the next several years. The dissolution of Marguerite's marriage helped strengthen the bond between mother and daughter.

To escape Houston's heat, Marguerite worked one summer in Boothbay Harbor, Maine, where she had fond memories from having spent two summers during college. While working as a cook's assistant at an inn, she met other artists who had come to work at a local art studio. "The Bay Street Studio changed my life … The people who frequented the inn were mostly New York artists and writers who escaped from their day jobs for two weeks to come to the coast of Maine to paint. Many lived and worked all year just to be able to come up and spend a couple of weeks painting and pursuing their passion."

During this summer Marguerite met Jud Strunk, a poet, performer, and musician with a small band. She decided to spend more time in Maine with Jud, who lived in a big log home in Eustis. "I still had my apartment in Houston and jobs I could go back to, so I commuted for a while, but then I just moved in. That's how I really got to know the interior of Maine and the mountains. Living with him was so peripatetic that it was hard to maintain a studio, but I really honed my figure-drawing skills, because I was constantly drawing members of the band and people sitting at concerts."

Marguerite was in Houston in 1981 when Jud was killed in a plane crash. "I thought that might end my time in Maine, but over the course of the next year I decided I not only missed being in Maine and the work I could do there, but also the out-of-doors and the friends I had there. So in 1982 I took a leave of absence from my job, packed my car with my paints and my fly rod and shotgun, drove to Maine, and rented a house from a friend in Eustis. I'm still here."

At first Marguerite eeked out a living doing graphic design and architectural renderings and painted in between. Then in 1988 she received a grant to the Vermont Studio Colony, working alongside twenty or so other artists. "It really did a lot to change my approach to how I was painting and how much time I was spending on it." Soon afterward, Brunswick gallery owner Ray Farrell took her on as one of his new artists and in 1989 gave Marguerite her first one-person show. "He started selling my work and doing well with it." As a result, she had to not only paint more but also think more about her work and the various series of pieces she wanted to present. The following year, after presenting a body of work to the Farnsworth Art Museum, she received a grant to paint at Corinna House on Monhegan, where she produced a large body of new work.

Marguerite's success was marred by the death of her mother in 1989. The death left a huge void, which is still there, but with it Marguerite came to realize that she had to make it on her own; she could no longer reach out to her mother for moral, emotional, or financial support. At the same time, this realization reinforced her awareness of her mother's traits that she wanted to emulate—the independence of spirit and the ability to take care of herself and live her own life.

Marguerite uses the landscape and the love of family and friends to reflect her sense of spirit and soul, which comes largely from nature. She wants her work to have a certain reverence. She wants her portrayal to be both austere and to have clarity. She wants it to reflect her personal beliefs in a set of values that we all live by.

Eustis, Maine

A passion for computers

JANET HARVIE

Portland, Maine   Born 1968

Founded a Web page design company

" **M**y mission, my passion, and one of my dreams is to make sure that everyone has Internet access and everyone has a computer that gives them these opportunities."

Janet has put together a nonprofit organization called Access Everyone. Its development board is working with the president of the University of Southern Maine on a pilot project with the Riley School, soliciting donations to refurbish and distribute computers to anyone who can't justify the cost and to give them free Internet access as well. The organization's team of developers wants to use this idea as a model at the state and local level, and perhaps an even higher one. "This will become the basis of a study on how access to the Internet benefits these families," says Janet. "I'd like to even the playing field in technology, working to break down the digital divide that you hear about. It can't happen without help."

As a young person, Janet had no particular goals. She enjoyed having a good time and didn't find college of any great interest. Because she grew up with two older brothers, and all the neighborhood children her age were boys, she did mostly "boy things." Her father was a pharmacist with strong entrepreneurial leanings. Her mother had a lot of energy. Janet believes she inherited some of all these traits. After her father sold his drugstore rather than lose it to increased competition, the family moved to Brunswick, where Janet finished high school. She went to college, but she liked to party more than study. So after a year she decided that it was a waste of money and took time off to do other things.

Most of her early work experiences were dead ends, although she

31

did learn to play the guitar and write song lyrics. Eventually she met a computer guru who let her play with his computers. She remembers being mesmerized, spending ten to twelve hours at a time on her knees in front of computers trying to figure out how they worked. She was so fascinated that she decided to pursue a career in that field.

She pestered *Casco Bay Weekly* for a job using computers, and they finally offered her an internship. Three months later they offered her a real job, which she held for two years. When her boss left, she took over that job in graphic design. There she also learned how to maintain Web sites. She worked long hours, not bothering to put in for overtime because she was learning so much. She realized that Web site design held great potential. The newspaper wasn't interested in a Web site, so she started freelancing.

Less than three years after Janet first discovered her passion for computers, she started her own Web design business. At first it was out of her basement. She called herself Tricycle Media because she had expected to have two partners. That didn't happen, so she was really a unicycle, but it didn't matter.

Developing a strong work ethic was new to Janet, and it excited her. She was proud of herself and how far she had come. After a few months, she leased a storefront in Portland, setting up the space herself. Her father cosigned a loan, using his pickup as collateral, partly for the funds to buy what she needed to fix the space, partly for a second computer. It showed her parents' faith in her, because if she failed, her father stood to lose his truck and with it a way to get to work. The first few months were difficult. Janet had to learn to sell her Web sites as well as design them, to be a bookkeeper and do all the other things necessary in a new business. After four months she had enough orders to hire a programmer, then a graphic designer. This is now the team that makes up Portland Websmith, which is off to a successful start.

Janet's advice to other young women starting out? "It doesn't take a four-year degree; it doesn't take a two-year degree; it doesn't take money; it doesn't take anything but a passion and an interest in what you want to do. A passion means a big enough interest to get you up in the morning without an alarm clock … and keep you going late."

Portland, Maine

One's prime is elusive. You little girls,
when you grow up, must be on the
alert to recognize your prime at
whatever time of your life it may occur.

— Muriel Spark

Succeeding in a male-dominated profession

KATHY OUELLETTE

Caribou, Maine   Born 1954
Owner, M. J. Ouellette & Daughters,
road & excavation contractor

"If there's a challenge out there, I want to go for it and see what it's
all about. When I was a little kid I'd ask my father about wanting
to be something, and he'd say, whatever you are, be a good one ...
This profession can't all be men. There's room for women too. For young
girls ... you can be anywhere you want to be ... Now you can be what
you want to be ... You've got to dare to dream."

The earth-moving business is among the most male-dominated professions. Yet at a bid meeting, Kathy says, "Don't give me the job
because I'm a woman. Give me this job because I'll do it well, and you'll
be glad you did. I'm no different than any man you'd hire. My equipment has no gender." Such forthrightness typifies her—that and her
obvious intelligence, energy, and self-confidence.

Kathy was born and raised in the Caribou area by independent-
minded parents. She says she has always been independent. "That's fundamental; if we wanted something we had to work for it." There were six
children, five of them girls. Because the family was poor, all were
encouraged to work. The children started picking potatoes when they
were five and worked as carhops and waitresses when they were older.
Kathy married right out of high school, had her first daughter at age
nineteen, and started working for a local bank shortly thereafter. At the
same time, she attended night school. A second daughter was born six
years later. The bank assigned her to various branches around Aroostook
County, and she eventually became assistant vice president.

During these years, Kathy and her husband purchased an earth-
moving business and bought a backhoe. Kathy ran the business and did
the bidding, bonding, and paperwork while her husband provided the
labor along with one other employee. Kathy's paycheck went back into
the business to pay the employee until the business started making

money. Then a serious car accident several years later changed her life. It was then that she decided she really wanted to make the business work. She quit her bank job and used the retirement fund she received to buy out her husband's share, thus putting all the responsibility for success squarely on her shoulders.

Today, Kathy's business involves grading and road building, culverts and drainage work, as well as septic systems and subdivision utilities. Her husband works for her, as do both daughters and her husband's brother. Their older daughter works mainly in the office, and the younger one works in the field in summer. Kathy does the takeoffs (measuring the amounts of cut and fill involved) and the bidding, secures an engineer for layouts, and does some field supervision. There are several full-time employees as well as extra help during the summer season. She looks forward to the time when one or both her daughters can assume more responsibility. In the meantime, Kathy is reaping the benefits of carrying out projects well—namely, greater acceptance by her customers. This has sometimes been grudging in a business dominated by men.

Describing one of her contracts, Kathy talks about being out in the woods along a fourteen-mile stretch of road where they replaced all the culverts. "Out in the woods at five in the morning, getting the equipment in place, laying out the cut for a culvert, staying ahead of the crew, only meeting a few pulp trucks going by, seeing a bear cub and its mother along the way, I was at peace, and I loved doing what I was doing. It doesn't get any better than that for me."

Kathy thrives on continual challenge. Her advice to anyone? "Challenge yourself ... there's no satisfaction from [taking] the easy path."

Caribou, Maine

If I have to, I can do anything.
I am strong, I am invincible,
I am woman.

— Helen Reddy

Radical political activist

KATHRYN McINNIS-MISENOR

Saco, Maine   Born 1958

Writer of national legislation for people with disabilities, director of Maine LEAP (mentoring young girls with disabilities)

Kathryn may be small and soft of voice, but she has a strong sense of justice. She believes passionately in changing the world for the better. Her words ring with the fervor of a dedicated radical. "I am a Marxist, and I believe in a socialized system that is opposed to capitalism and to the control of resources by a few people. I believe in the distribution of wealth, resources, and knowledge."

Kathryn has backed her fervor with action for many years. She started in the early 1980s as a community organizer in Portland—organizing labor, environmental activities, and political action supporting protection for people with disabilities. Using the Maine Human Rights Act as a base, she worked with Tom Andrews, among others, to sue the cities of South Portland, Portland, and Westbrook for the right of the disabled to have access to public transportation. They won at the state supreme court level on the basis that separate was not equal.

Then they sued the United States Department of Transportation and President George Bush and Elizabeth Dole as their representatives at the federal level for failure to comply on constitutional grounds. Again they won, in the United States Third Circuit Court of Appeals. Their efforts made accessible transportation a fundamental right. With another group, Kathryn helped write the Americans With Disabilities Act (ADA), which became law in 1990.

Not only was Kathryn heavily involved in pushing for disability rights legislation, she got her undergraduate degree in social work at the

University of Southern Maine followed by a master's degree from Boston College in social work. In her twenty years of organizing, she has worked with a variety of organizations, including the African National Congress and IRATE among others. She is now the director of Maine LEAP, a mentoring program for girls and women with disabilities. She is also married and has a young daughter.

How did she achieve this extraordinary drive? Her mother persuaded Kathryn that she could do anything she set out to do. From the time of Kathryn's diagnosis of rheumatoid arthritis at age six and her required use of a wheelchair from the age of ten, her mother became her coach and cheerleader, saying no to the doctors wanting to give her steroids because they might cause infertility. She was sure that her daughter would marry someday and have children. "My mother was really strong about saying, this is what life is going to be like five years, ten years, and fifty years down the road. She was very much focused on never giving up on my potential, which was a blessing, because I was disabled when I went to school. When I was in the fourth grade, they would not allow me to continue because of safety concerns. My mom fought the school, tutored me, then hired a tutor and forced the school to pay for it." For high school, her mother fought to get her into Thornton Academy in Saco, which Kathryn completed in two years.

Growing up was emotionally painful for Kathryn. She was seen as different, as not belonging. Other children, she says, made her feel as though she stuck out like a sore thumb. As a result, she became terribly shy. But the rejection had another effect: "I was damned determined to graduate with my class and to be at the ceremony."

Kathryn says that her mother, Jean McInnis, is "a real strong character. She's from an Irish working class family and very independent. I think my radicalism comes from her. She was always busy with community service or organizing."

Kathryn's oldest sister became involved in politics when she worked on Robert Kennedy's campaign. Thus politics and community service were very much a part of Kathryn's growing up, as was mediation. Even as a small child, she would lie on the ground and separate insects that were fighting. This extended to mediating fights among her siblings, to determine where justice should lie.

The character of mother as well as daughter was revealed at the signing of the Americans With Disabilities Act. The seven authors of the bill were told by President Bush that they could each bring two people to the signing. The authors of the bill looked at one another. Thousands of people would be affected by this legislation, and the president was telling them that they could bring only two people each? Kathryn describes the event: "We met with President Bush and said, if you're going to sign this bill, you're going to do it on our terms. So he agreed to open it up, and we had hundreds of people invited. I took my mom and Tom Andrews. As Kathryn commiserated later with Tom Andrews about hating the compromises they had to make so the bill would pass, her mother said, "For Christ's sake, isn't it enough for you kids that you have helped write the biggest piece of civil rights legislation since the voting rights act? You sit here complaining ... when you should be figuring out what to do to make this piece of paper work."

Kathryn's current role as director of Maine LEAP illustrates her dedication to seeing that certain groups of people are not left behind. Still in its infancy, LEAP was organized by a small group of women with disabilities—to match girls with disabilities with women who have related problems. Says Kathryn, the women could tell the girls, "You are who you are inside, and you need to determine what your potential is. You will always meet people who will tell you no, that isn't your potential. But then [you] realize that when they say 'no, you can't do it,' they probably mean they can't ... Know that you can do it until you have proven to yourself that you can't."

As sharp, feisty, and independent as Kathryn is, she constantly battles the perception of her as being asexual, even after her marriage and pregnancy. When a grocery clerk noticed her engagement ring and asked if it was her grandmother's, Kathryn countered, "No, it's my engagement ring!" A stranger behind her in the checkout line patted her on the shoulder and said, "Isn't it nice that you found a boy to marry you and give up sex." I said, "What makes you think he's taking care of me? In fact he's working part time, and I'm putting his ass through school [while] I'm working full time and finishing my graduate work."

When Kathryn was pregnant, people would ask if she'd been artificially inseminated. Kathryn's husband, who is not disabled, would respond, "No, we did it the old-fashioned way."

Kathryn is a beacon who tells people with disabilities that they can achieve much more than they ever imagined, including living full lives.

Portland, Maine

Much-admired advocate for women and the disabled

PENNY PLOURDE

Augusta, Maine   Born 1954

*Heads Civil Rights Division of Maine's
Department of Transportation*

"I couldn't run, couldn't jump, couldn't play with kids in the traditional way, so the way I made it work for me was through the power of language—through becoming more outward within. I am a great extrovert ... I love sharing because it empowers me ... It's good for my ego, and in some way that may be the message."

Penny is so strong-minded and strong-willed and has such a compelling personality that you may forget that she was a spina bifida baby. Although she uses a wheelchair, she seems to live her own life pretty much on her own terms. She drives a hand-operated van, lives by herself, travels by air when the occasion demands, and calls on other people with disabilities to give them support. She seems happiest when empowering others to do more.

How did Penny gain the strength to overcome her physical handicap and find the inner confidence to act in ways that make others treat her as they would anyone? Raised primarily in Fort Kent, the oldest of three daughters, she learned to live not only with her disability and the lack of available care locally, but with the fact that she was the first obviously disabled child in the community. She had endured more than thirty operations by the time she was twelve. That was when she saw a description of herself in a textbook; she was referred to as a spina bifida child—a box-like figure with protruding arms and legs. It devastated her because it was not the image she wanted to portray. More important, it shocked her into thinking about who she was and who she wanted to become. With her parents' support, Penny essentially told the doctors

43

that there wouldn't be any more operations, that they had made all the improvements they were going to make. She decided that the rest had to come from her; she would use leg braces and crutches, or a wheelchair.

This act of independence was the start of her resolution to live her own life as much as possible. Her school told her she couldn't attend because she represented a risk. She told the school there was nothing wrong with her intellect. They offered a compromise: tutoring. Her counter compromise: attending another school. She went to Mount Merici Academy, a Catholic boarding school in Waterville, and graduated in 1972. Back at home she enrolled in the University of Maine at Fort Kent. Through all of this, Penny's parents were supportive, as were her two sisters. Her parents wanted the girls to have access to jobs other than picking potatoes or working in the woods. Her father managed a men's clothing store, her mother worked for a local mental health agency, and her sister Terry owned a children's clothing store. The entire family worked.

Before leaving college, Penny became a volunteer in the 1978 gubernatorial campaign. She found that she liked planting the seed and letting it grow, and before long she had a full-time paid position. Her candidate won. Penny moved to Augusta and worked for a few years for the Department of Labor before being offered her current position as Coordinator of Civil Rights in the Department of Transportation. This has become her platform to help others and make things happen. This is what has allowed her to become a strong, independent voice and force— first, to help women and minorities gain economic parity in employment for state contracts; second, to bring the department into the twenty-first century with respect to services and employment for people with disabilities. Where do you put a streetlight with an audible signal? How do you make sure that the ferries, buses, and other mass transit facilities are accessible to those with disabilities? This is Penny's real job, and she has found that it takes much more than words—it takes design and layout, and educating communities by her example of what it's like to have a disability in this century.

Penny learned long ago that her success and her ability to remain fully functioning as an independent woman depended at least in part on her ability to move others to see her condition in ways that would not make them feel sorry for her or attempt to help her more than necessary. A few years ago, coming out of the State House, she fell down the stone front steps. A group of state VIPs was standing there when it happened.

As she started to roll down the steps, unable to stop, what kept going through her mind was how to make light of the incident so those around her wouldn't feel the need to be overly protective. She says that when someone came to help her up, "I laughed and noted that I must have looked pretty funny bouncing down the stairs like a ball."

Most of us have little comprehension of what Penny Plourde has been through. Did the fact that she suffered and survived set the stage for becoming a strong, independent woman? Or was it there from the beginning? Although she grew up among strong women, including her mother, and had her father's support, she is living proof of the power of the human spirit to achieve a full life against many obstacles.

She says she never wants to be an enabler. "I always want others to be strong enough to fight." Although the disabled may find resources here or there, the first step, she points out, is finding things they can do for themselves to take control of their lives. "That's what I do and that's my life."

Augusta, Maine

Valuing integrity over security

MURIEL CURTIS

Liberty, Maine   Born 1954
Jill of many trades, lover of music

"I see myself as very much a woman, a complete woman, and very much a whole human being. I'll try my hand at anything. If I fail, well shucky darn! I'll pick myself up and try again."

To paraphrase a song title from the *Sound of Music*, "How do you solve a problem like Muriel?" How do you hold a moonbeam in your hand? She's irrepressible; she's a fount of constant good humor; she's a bundle of energy; she will take on any job and just do it; she knows how to squeeze a dollar until it squeals—and then squeeze it again. And she is one of the most completely independent individuals you're ever apt to meet. One of her most often repeated sayings is, "I love my life." And she seems to really mean it.

Muriel grew up in a working-class neighborhood in Cambridge, Massachusetts. She says proudly that she is a bastard and has the papers to prove it. She learned that her mother often played the helpless female when she was perfectly capable of doing the job herself. Muriel's childhood reaction to her mother's wiles, coupled with the fact that she was punished for doing "boy kinds of things," caused her to rebel, to actively discard most female behavior and adopt male attitudes. She was an overachiever; she knew she was bright, brighter than her parents, and decided early that she did not want to be like them. Despite being dyslexic, she graduated from college and later earned a master's degree. She went around with groups, never dating. Along the way, she developed a love of music, particularly voice, one of her defining passions.

Money was tight when Muriel was young, and her mother worked summers on Hermit Island in Casco Bay to get the children out of the city. It was here that Muriel developed a love of the ocean and of boats, which would become the focus of many of her occupations as, she says, she "bebopped around the world." It was after college and a stint at teaching that she began to "mess about in boats" in a serious way. For ten years or more she took on many jobs in the United States and Europe, sailing on traditional vessels, first as galley girl, then working her way up to first mate. Later she spent two years as a rigger on a three-masted bark with twenty-nine sails—a lot of rigging. While the male crew members would haul the courses, it was Muriel who went aloft to set or furl the topsails and, even higher up, the royals. In Europe she worked with charter companies and managed one for a while despite the reluctance of many Europeans to have a woman on board, let alone having her give the orders. In the off season she took on almost any job that came along. She picked potatoes in Scotland and hauled the creel on a prawn fishing boat. She says the boat work was so hard she couldn't eat enough to keep from losing weight. She worked at farming, nursing, and boat maintenance. Along the way she received her hundred-ton captain's license.

Eventually Muriel came back to the United States and got her master's degree in education. She was drawn to Maine by the invitation of a friend and her fond summer memories. After working on a farm in Montville, she settled in Liberty, where she managed to scrape together enough money for a down payment on a piece of land. She resurrected the shell of a small cabin, put it on a foundation, and finished it inside and out. She built an outhouse, a deck, and a woodshed, all from scrounged lumber. Her cabin has no electricity, no indoor plumbing, and no telephone, but it is cozy and insulated. It is more than half a mile from her nearest neighbor and more than two miles through the woods to the house of a blind neighbor, where she trades a weekly bath for doing some chores. She loves her lifestyle, although the community may be too small to hold her for long. She has big ideas. And she has a derelict Friendship sloop that was given to her to fix up. The list goes on.

To support herself and to allow the luxury of teaching music in the local school and church, Muriel has held a variety of jobs, including teaching inmates at the Belfast jail to use computers, helping young women get their equivalency certificates, and painting and repairing boats. More recently she has worked at the Atlantic Challenge Foundation, helping to collect and organize information on boatbuilding techniques and materials. She produced and directed the Rockland Sea

Ceilidh, a music festival that hosted Pete Seeger in 1999 and Gordon Bok in 2000 and again in 2001.

Muriel's lifestyle has left her little chance for serious romance while she traveled around the world. Additionally, her penchant for competing for male-dominated jobs has resulted in her taking on a more masculine demeanor—an approach to life that she's now modifying as she pursues her love of teaching music. This attitude and her experiences are evident in her overriding credo: "I will never trade any part of my soul for security. If I'm with a man, I want to be myself—none of this trying to make me into something I'm not." Nevertheless, Muriel has had two major love affairs, neither of which resulted in marriage. With Muriel, it would be a mistake to make any predictions for the future. She's very apt to fool you.

Camden, Maine

Independent adventurer and traveller

ANNELIESE FRANCIS

Stockton Springs, Maine   Born 1959
Long-distance trucker, single mom

"**D**on't let your fears keep you from doing things ... fear of change, fear of trying something new, fear of failure, or fear of rejection. Don't worry about all that stuff. Do it anyway, just to try it, and if it doesn't work out, do something else."

Anneliese's competence and directness are instantly obvious. It's apparent upon meeting her that she enjoys people and feels comfortable in almost any situation. It isn't a shock to learn that she drove eighteen-wheelers cross-country for ten years, mostly by herself. When not driving or caring for her eleven-year-old son, she's apt to be on her motorcycle or in her canoe.

Her strong independent streak was nurtured by several things: growing up in a military family that moved often, by her mother letting her do almost anything without supervision from a very early age, and by her father wanting to exert too much control, which made Anneliese constantly fight for more freedom.

She was born in England, where her father, who was on a tour of duty, had married a German woman with an infant girl—Anneliese's half sister. Soon the family was moved to Springfield, Massachusetts, then Pease Air Force Base in New Hampshire, then Stockton Springs, Maine, where they bought a house and stayed until Anneliese was five. Several moves later they were in Europe again, this time in Belgium, where they spent several years. Here, Anneliese began taking trips around Europe with friends.

During this period the battle of wills between Anneliese and her father became so serious that whenever her mother left to visit family in Germany, Anneliese stayed with friends, telling her father that she wasn't

coming home until her mother returned. A solution to the constant battle
of wills presented itself when she was seventeen and moved in with her
cousin's family in Stockton Springs, where she finished her high school
education.

After high school, Anneliese began what was to become her career—
first she rode with a trucker, and when she was invited to drive, she discovered that dealing with a thirteen-speed transmission came easily to
her. So she kept driving with that driver to a variety of destinations.
After returning to more humdrum jobs and working in construction for a
while, Anneliese finally decided to try to get her trucker's license. At
nineteen she was too young, so she enrolled at a technical school, where
she learned to rebuild transmissions and diesel engines. She also learned
two valuable lessons: Because women usually have smaller hands than
men do, it was easy to get her hands into difficult-to-reach places; and
as the only woman in a large group of men, she learned how to take the
kidding and comments with a smile on her face.

At twenty-one, Anneliese finished driving school, received her trucker's license, and took a job with a Scarborough firm. "Wow, what a trip
that was," she says. "I didn't have a clue about anything." But she persevered, hauling mainly bulk paper, finding her own loads as an independent driver, traveling as far south as Florida and west to Ohio—hard
work but on her own time with good pay. Being a woman was also probably more help than hindrance, because she almost always had assis-
tance with unloading. Two years later, when she was in Florida driving
for a concrete company, she teamed up with a man and drove with him
for three years. They separated when she realized that he was too posses-
sive, and she went back to driving alone. She was given her own truck
and traveled to every major city in the United States and parts of
Canada. When one company folded, she hooked up with another, always
getting a job, partly because she was a woman and partly because she
had an excellent driving record. She had two other points in her favor—
she didn't mind driving at night and could go long hours without sleep.
She didn't have a lot of problems with harassment, but when it did come
she usually got help from other truckers who were friends. She handled
one incident by herself: As the harasser tried to climb in the door of her
truck, she pulled away, opened the door he was hanging on to, slammed
on the brakes, and watched him fly to the ground.

At the age of twenty-eight, Anneliese had a child (she had wanted
to become a mother) and moved back to Stockton Springs more or less

permanently. Although that stopped her regular driving, when her son was old enough to stay with a sitter, she hired out as a relief driver. She also hauled mice out of Jackson Labs in Bar Harbor, a good fill-in job. Then she started working in the office of the Belfast Dance Studio and after a while began running the office.

Anneliese's life on the road has come to an end as she has become a mother, though it is a choice she gladly made, for her son is her central focus until he is grown and on his own. But the chance to travel remains a dream for the future. For now, she is satisfied with the chances she has to ride her motorcycle or get outside, and she continues to live by her motto: "Variety is the spice of life, but moderation is the key. Do everything. Just don't overdo it."

Camden, Maine

Pursuing a passion for helping women

KARIN ANDERSON

Portland, Maine   Born 1957
Director of Maine Women's Fund

When Karin was thirteen years old, her mother and father separated. Karin watched her mother, with whom she was very close, come apart with the realization of how much of her identity was tied up in the man she had married. It devastated Karin, the eldest child, to learn how dependent her mother was on another person. Karin, who was just figuring out what it meant to be a woman, made up her mind that she "was never going to let that happen to me. I didn't need a man. I really didn't care if I ever got married." Her decision influenced many of the choices she made as a young adult.

This story has more than one happy ending. Karin's parents did not divorce. They reconciled their differences and have had a relatively happy marriage. Karin, meanwhile, never stopped striving for her independence. She pursued an international summer exchange program when she was sixteen. This experience fostered an interest in languages, resulting in a decision to major in international relations in college. From there she went directly to graduate school for Latin American studies in Washington, D.C.

Washington opened Karin's eyes to a world beyond California, where she had grown up, and she loved it. At the same time she discovered that her language skills weren't strong enough for her to become an interpreter, and besides, her interests and ambitions went further. She started working for nonprofit organizations doing international exchange and/or health work, although she again found that she wasn't able to make the desired impact. In Washington she became active in volunteer work, usually with women's organizations. She became a board member of Planned Parenthood. She became interested in the refugee community and got involved in raising money specifically for women in refugee camps, discovering in the process that she had a natural talent for fund-raising.

The second happy ending to Karin's early experiences came when she was thirty. She married a man she met while working on a freelance fund-raising assignment. A year later they had a daughter. Although Karin's prophesy about not needing a man and not getting married came to naught, her resolve to live an independent life remained. Karin and her husband built an independent marriage—committed to each other but allowing each to lead a separate life. They maintained common goals for the family, but they pursued separate interests. Karin's was consulting, particularly fund-raising. She realized how empowering it is to be good at raising money. Combining this with her love of women's affairs, she began to direct her skills, which made her feel truly able to make a difference.

It was Karin's daughter who had the greatest influence on the family's next big decision—where to live. As her daughter reached school age, Karin and her husband decided to relocate to Maine, where the schools were safer and the quality of life was more to their liking. Because they were both consulting, they could live almost anywhere.

Their arrival in Portland in 1993 coincided with the Maine Women's Fund's search for a new director. Although Karin didn't have established contacts in her new community for raising money, she did offer strong fund-raising skills plus a passion for helping women. It seemed to be one of those matches preordained to succeed.

Along with the organization, Karin has come to understand why a number of women don't become all they might be. Some of the reasons are built into the messages that girls receive early in life: They have to be pretty, they have to be thin, they shouldn't appear smarter than boys, they have to work harder than men to do a man's job. In the absence of messages to the contrary, it is too easy for girls to accept the negative messages and to stop trying to reach their full potential. For this reason, the Maine Women's Fund supports work with girls in a vulnerable age group—ten to twelve years old. The Fund gives other messages to girls: They are strong; they can do anything.

Karin's success derives not just from her friendliness, intelligence, and enthusiasm, all of which are readily apparent, but from an innate ability to gather people into her sphere and have them want to help her achieve her goals. She is not shy about saying what she wants to accomplish. She has the ability of the skillful executive to work toward building consensus in selling her ideas so that they become the ideas of others as well.

Karin's dream—to do more writing on women's issues—meshes with her advice to young women: "The most important piece of advice that I would offer a young woman is that her options and her choices are limitless, that the only person who puts limits on her is herself. This doesn't mean that all choices are equally easy. But there is no reason why any girl can't be thinking about being anything when she grows up … Education is very important; life experiences are very important; knowing as many different kinds of people as you have the opportunity to know is very enriching, because you don't know what life is going to bring. New doors open new pathways, and we should always be open for that."

Since this profile was first written, there has been one major change in Karin's life—the decision by both her husband and herself to separate and seek a divorce. Karin's daughter is now the same age Karin was when her parents separated. But because Karin knows who she is, and is comfortable with the decision, it may prove less troubling for her daughter than it did for her.

Portland, Maine

Boat captain, educator, creating order out of chaos

CATE CRONIN

Rockport, Maine   Born 1957
Director, Atlantic Challenge Foundation

Cate Cronin was eighteen when she dropped out of college to work on boats. She worked as a galley person for an established Camden windjammer for two summers, which was a somewhat ordered situation. Then she jumped into chaos, working on another schooner for someone starting out with no systems in place. Why? She didn't have the answer but kept on doing it. She completed the Outward Bound course, taking one of their open boats from Florida to Hurricane Island, off the Maine coast—rowing and sailing for 2,000 miles. She got her captain's license and became intrigued by the *Clearwater*, a 110-foot Hudson River sloop replica sailing out of New York to do environmental teaching. She worked aboard when she could, one time for a three-month stretch. She worked on big boats in the Caribbean in winter, then came back up north in summer. Suddenly one winter day, she received a telegram from the captain of the *Clearwater* saying he wanted her to be the boat's next captain. She was twenty-three years old. She'd have to be there on April 1. He'd provide a month of transition, then she'd be on her own. She agonized for days thinking she wasn't ready, then accepted and left for New York.

She arrived to find an older crew, mostly men. A few women also helped care for the boat, and did so with great skill. The trips were the start of an environmental education program for school kids, which involved taking out students and teachers in the morning, and again in the afternoon, then traveling through the night to the next town to do it again, over and over. There was no home port. So after the boat arrived in a town, Cate would jump off and find a telephone to arrange schedules, parts, supplies, new crew, new teachers, new students, hiring,

59

maintenance, yard work—the myriad of things essential to keeping a boat sailing and seaworthy. She became the queen of logistics.

That was Cate's story for ten years—five before and five after she took over the *Clearwater*. It meant no personal entanglements, because, as she says, that wouldn't have been appropriate. It also meant a great deal of visibility and focus on her as a woman captain rather than on the program they were trying to promote. To attempt to deflect this and become more media savvy, Cate turned to Toshi Seeger, Pete Seeger's wife (the couple who put together the foundation to build the *Clearwater*), who told her, "Look at this list of women who've sailed their ships home for their husbands or done some fascinating trips themselves. Throw that right back at them. Say you're not the first woman captain. Say you're following this line of women who've done it when they needed to." Says Cate, "Today I can thank the women who've paved the way, from suffrage to the other focal points of our history, who made it possible for me to have a job like this on my own merit."

Sailing and navigating a boat as big as the *Clearwater* is not child's play. The term jibing means changing course so the mainsail is swung from one side of the boat to the other while still heading downwind. Even on dinghies, this can be difficult if the wind is blowing hard. On a craft the size of the *Clearwater*, with a boom seventy-eight feet in length, two to three times the diameter of a large telephone pole, and weighing as much as a medium-size car, jibing requires knowledge and perfect timing to bring it off without doing considerable damage.

What helped Cate develop so much self-confidence at a young age? Her early family life, with art- and music-oriented parents, helped. The second of five children, she grew up in Bangor at a time when city children had a great deal of freedom. She and her siblings rode their bikes in the country and later earned summer cash by washing dishes at the Lobster Pound in Lincolnville. Here she soon realized that if she was going to be paid to do dishes, she'd much rather do them on a schooner. Her grandmother also influenced Cate. In the days when it was unusual for a woman to have a career, Cate's grandmother ran the nonprofit children's home made immortal in John Irving's book *The Cider House Rules*.

In 1982, Cate married crew member Peter Webb, returned to college and received her degree, then went on to the Harvard Graduate School of Education, where she rubbed shoulders with many senior educators returning for advanced degrees. During the summer, she went to sea. This pattern continued for eight years while her husband taught at the Landing School in Kennebunkport. During this time she tried to decide whether or not it was possible to reconcile mainstream education with the various "downstream" alternatives that she had been connected with. Through this process, she began to learn how nonprofit organizations run or don't run well.

After moving to Rockport in 1990, Cate answered an ad for the job of Director of the Maine Island Trail Association. This gave her the opportunity to run a nonprofit organization, starting with it as one segment of the Island Institute, working on its growth, then seeing it become a freestanding organization. In this she was aided by Karen Stimpson (see page 63), who acted as trail director, then took over Cate's job when she left in 1997. During this period Cate had two children and led a somewhat normal home life.

Since 1997, Cate has been Director of the Atlantic Challenge Foundation in Rockland, testing her abilities—well recognized by the board—to lead skillfully by gaining consensus and creating order from chaos. She has helped the organization grow and move into new quarters as well as become immersed in the continuing necessity of all nonprofits—raising money to run the organization. She has freed up the prior director, Lance Lee, to do what he does best, which is to inspire young people to reach beyond anything they thought possible. Perhaps her biggest success has been in recognizing that a facility such as an apprentice shop has to broaden its appeal by becoming involved in other activities that in turn increase the support base. This has meant developing programs such as the after-school boatbuilding project, the community sailing project, and seminars for the public entitled "All Things Nautical."

Cate has managed to juggle the multiple requirements of marriage, children, and careers, including those that have taken her away from home for long stretches of time. Gender is not an issue with her. Using a leadership technique that stresses consensus and avoids confrontation, she evokes an optimistic, energetic attitude that seems to say that anything and everything is possible.

Camden, Maine

A passion for the water and conservation

KAREN STIMPSON

Portland, Maine   Born 1951

Director of Maine Island Trail Association

66 I've lived a life charmed by good fortune, good luck, good parenting, and good environment. So I feel like a bit of a jerk saying this,
but I do believe that everyone—especially women—has at their
fingertips the ability to move in any direction they want. It's fear that
holds us back. If you can recognize that and believe—just for a moment
put aside the fear and believe—that you can create your own destiny,
you can create the world you want. Then you can look back on a life
that you really feel good about ... One of the things I can honestly say is,
if I die tomorrow, I've denied myself nothing. This isn't about self-indul-
gence. It's been about being true to my own compass course and living
every moment as though it would be my last."

Karen Stimpson backs up her words with experience. She was one
of the two women on the yacht described in *The Perfect Storm* who was
picked out of the ocean by the U.S. Coast Guard. She won't say much
about this other than that the wind was blowing about sixty knots and
the seas were running forty feet. Then she adds, "In 1973, when I was
twenty-one, I was in a storm that was worse; it just didn't happen to
make it into a best-seller. That storm set my parameter for extremes, and
everything in between until *The Perfect Storm* seemed like child's play
by comparison. If I hadn't gone through that experience in 1973, each
bigger wave, each scarier experience would have put the fear of God in
me, and I might have been less inclined to go back out there. But having
hit the mother lode of bad conditions when I was twenty-one and inde-
structible, once I got over that, I was back on the water again."

Karen delivers boats as a sideline—something she takes on occasionally because of her love of being on the water. This is where she

recharges her emotional batteries. "Being on a boat on the water by myself settles me in ways that nothing else can. I believe that when I'm on shore, what's important is to do as good a job as I can at whatever I'm doing. I try to do it all. I try to have a social life as well. I just spin wheels; I'm like a gerbil in one of those little runs. But as soon as I get away from shore, I let it all go. I'm peaceful, contemplative, slow. All of a sudden real values in life come back, and I'm happy. It's my penultimate place. I don't have a religious context, but if I'm alone on watch on deck … I have a sense of being connected to something. I couldn't define what it is except that everything is exactly as it should be."

Karen's primary job combines two of her major passions: a love of the water and her strong conservation ethic. She has directed the Maine Island Trail Association (MITA) for more than ten years. Her office is on Union Wharf in Portland, and her home is aboard one of her boats, the *Junniatta*, a 1920s motor cruiser that she keeps tied up nearby. MITA was formed to provide access to wild islands along the Maine coast so that users of small boats could visit and camp on them. The initial thrust was to build membership and, in so doing, build a constituency for stewardship and concern for these islands. The organization has proved itself to be almost too successful. The number of protected islands has grown to 118, and the number of people visiting the islands has grown to the point where MITA now has to manage access to avoid destruction of fragile areas. Two hundred volunteers help maintain the sites. For Karen, the fascinating and rewarding task is providing access to wonderful places that people would otherwise not see and at the same time managing that access to protect the environment.

When Karen was first retained by MITA, it was part of the Island Institute. Cate Cronin was brought in at the same time as Executive Director, and Karen became Trail Director with her own separate office in Portland and her own fund-raising base. Soon MITA was broken off as a separate organization, and when Cate left in 1997, Karen took over as Executive Director.

Where did Karen develop her love of the water, strong feeling for conservation, and strong independent streak? When she was still a baby, her parents bought land in Wilderness Cove on Sebago Lake, where her mother built a good portion of their camp while her father worked overtime so they could afford it. At the age of five, Karen was given a fourteen-foot aluminum boat and a small outboard motor. Her father's admonition was, "It's yours, but if you break it, you fix it." Karen broke the motor repeatedly. Her father didn't fix it for her; he fixed it with her, so she eventually learned to fix it herself. As Karen says, "The stereotyping wasn't there. Even though I was a female, I was operating a boat at a very young age, to the admiration of all the girls around the lake."

Karen spent summers and weekends for six months of every year at the lake until she left home to attend college. During this period, she watched the area become built up with houses on little hundred-foot lots all around the lake. She watched Wilderness Cove become developed. She watched while the moose and turtles and other animal life began to disappear.

It was these experiences that gave Karen her undying love of being on the water. The destruction of the wilderness instilled in her a conservation ethic—a compulsion—that has driven her to pursue conservation activities within her work and beyond.

What helped establish Karen's strong independent streak? Her family had high expectations for their daughter as well as themselves. Her mother in particular was assertive, outspoken, and able to fix things herself. As Karen says, "What she didn't create in her own life, she was determined I would create in mine. The message was very loud and clear: Don't let anyone close a door in your face; kick it open. If anyone ever tells you [that] you can't do something, knock them down and go right ahead and prove you can. And don't ever let any guy make you secondary."

When Karen was thirteen, her older brother, a helicopter pilot, was killed in the Vietnam War. The resulting protectiveness of her mother only helped to solidify Karen's determination to be independent. "It became a theme in my life to get myself to a place where I would have complete freedom and independence. And it is still important today. I've created for myself a very busy and happy life. My moments of loneliness are few and far between. This doesn't provide much incentive to get involved in a relationship. Add to this my overriding love of being able to go wherever and whenever I want and not have to answer to anyone. Plus being headstrong anyway—it's not a great formula for relationships. Although I've had some great ones ... they haven't led to marriage. There's a lot more compromising that the guy wants than I'm willing to do."

Karen's path from growing up and leaving home to becoming the director of MITA is a circuitous one that provides more insights into who she is. She obtained a degree in graphic design from the Museum School of Fine Arts and at Simmons College. Afterward she worked for *Sail Magazine* as a graphic designer. At twenty-one she bought her first boat, a twenty-five-foot sloop. Wanting to sail more than she could while working for a magazine, she took a job teaching filmmaking, photography, and graphic design at Wellesley College, where she stayed for five years. Wanting to do more sailing and still earn a living, she came back to Portland to enter a program at Southern Maine Technical College teaching African Americans and women to become merchant marine officers. By the time she graduated with her third mate's license, the bottom had dropped out of U.S. merchant fleet opportunities, so she went back to graphic design. Only this time she set up her own freelance practice on board another boat she had bought, the *Junniatta*, which she has turned into her home in Portland Harbor. As Karen says, "[My business] was very successful and made a ton of money, so I lost my incentive to get back on the water." By the time there were jobs again in the merchant marine, she had gone to work for MITA.

Karen's dreams for her career have changed somewhat over the years. A long-term dream has been to sail around the world. To help make that happen, she bought yet another boat, a Westsail 32. Another dream is to write. Originally she wanted to combine sailing and writing, but this too may be changing. Still another dream is to have a large parcel of land on which to take in unwanted and hurt animals, care for them, and find homes for them. In some ways this is close to what Karen is currently doing; she and some other users of Union Wharf take care of a large population of stray cats that inhabit the wharves. They provide food and some shelter and try to find homes for the animals.

Karen's advice is to spend time by yourself in nature. "Being alone like that for a period of time—days and nights at a time—will provide you with the opportunity to look back into yourself, shake yourself down and give you the inner strength to fight later on. If possible it should be done outside of any existing program, on your own devices, in a place where there is no insurance of your safety and you have to become totally self-reliant. I am not recommending putting yourself at serious risk—just to be in a place where you gain confidence and the ability to fight if required, the ability to stand true to your own belief system."

Aboard *Junniatta* in Portland Harbor, Maine

Where I was born and where and
how I lived is unimportant. It is what
I have done with where I have lived
that should be of interest.

— Georgia O'Keeffe

Skillful organizer and motivator

SHEILA TASKER

Tenants Harbor, Maine   Born 1952

*Former President and CEO of Center for
Maine Contemporary Art*

Sheila was seventeen and engaged to marry after she graduated from high school. She was in love but had some niggling doubts. One morning she woke up thinking she didn't want to live the life her mother did—just keeping house and raising children. There had to be more to life than that. Her father had always said she could do or be anything she wanted to be, so she decided to break her engagement. It created an awful scene with her mother, but she didn't give in. She had always been headstrong and not inclined to cave in after taking a position. Her mother was so upset that she told Sheila to leave the house for good. So she did.

The second of six children, Sheila was her father's favorite and went almost everywhere with him. The family had moved from Maine to Connecticut to earn a better living, and after leaving home, Sheila immediately got a job with a major insurance company in Hartford, becoming one of the thousands of clerks who work in such businesses. After being there for about six months, she asked a question and was informed that it wasn't her job to ask questions—to simply do what she was told. At lunchtime, Sheila walked across the street to a big bank that was hiring for several kinds of positions. She was shown more rows of clerks. She looked at another bank that had a training program for customer service representatives. She signed up immediately, becoming one of the first such representatives of the second largest bank in Connecticut. She never looked back.

69

Sheila returned to college part-time in addition to her work for the bank, graduating summa cum laude twelve years later. At the bank, she moved from service representative to a management training program, and from that into managing various branches of the bank. She learned that management was really all the same, regardless of the size of the firm. The difference was only in the number of zeros in the year-end figures. Then she started to wonder whether this was what she wanted to do for the rest of her life.

Throughout her estrangement with her mother, Sheila maintained her close relationship with her father, meeting him surreptitiously. After a year of silence her mother began to speak to her again, although their relationship has remained somewhat strained. When Sheila was thirty, she met and married Rick Tasker, whom she describes as a wonderful man and her best friend. Early on they decided not to have children, instead choosing to focus on their work and on each other.

Sheila became head of the private banking department, then was made vice president of the bank. But along the way she figured out that what made her happy was taking an idea from its inception and implementing it; when it became a maintenance situation, her interest waned. That's why she became bored with banking and decided it was time to do something different.

The decision to leave the Hartford area was not difficult, because Sheila and her husband had a vacation house in Maine. But the lack of other opportunities put her back in banking. In Maine, she stayed in it for five more years, until she had developed contacts in the area. One of them was Maine Coast Artists in Rockport (now the Center for Maine Contemporary Art), where she was hired as development director. When the gallery launched its capital campaign, she resigned her job to avoid a conflict of interests, then was retained as a consultant to run the campaign. With the completion of the campaign in 1997, she was approached to become president and CEO of the organization, the job she held until the summer of 2002.

What makes Sheila such an outstanding person is the sum of her many strengths. She is blessed with unusual intelligence. Whereas many bright people see several sides of a subject and wind up vacillating, Sheila hears all the views—and in fact tends to actively reach out to make sure that various positions are heard—but is quick to reach a decision and act on it. She has a lot of energy and gets a lot done. She can look honestly at herself, at who she is and what she wants to be. At the same time she seems able to swallow her wants in order to carry out whatever unpleasant tasks need doing. Gender is a nonissue. She could be a role model for anyone looking to become an executive.

Sheila's vision and her credo for herself are essentially the same— "to make sure I instill that same sense of being true to yourself in absolutely everybody I come in contact with. I want to create an environment wherever I am that allows people to be the best at whatever they choose to be best at."

Camden, Maine

Always working "because not working is lazy"

LYNN BROMLEY

South Portland, Maine   Born 1951

Social worker, psychotherapist, activist in women's affairs,
newly elected state senator

What makes Lynn Bromley run? Seemingly unsatisfied with her many roles in life, she wanted to run for the state legislature. Again. The first time she lost narrowly to a three-time incumbent, garnering 47 percent of the vote. The second time she ran against someone new and believed she had a good chance of winning. "I want to say I'm in the catbird seat," she said, "except there hasn't been a Democrat in this seat for thirty years ... I think people are hungry for community, yet tired of what they see of the political process, and I absolutely believe that I can do it differently and better ... " And she won handily in the 2000 election.

In addition to being a therapist in a group practice in Portland, she has been director of the Center for Diversity/Gender Equity at Southern Maine Technical College (SMTC), a job that she had to give up after her election. She is also a member of numerous boards and advisory councils and writes new legislation in the areas of her interest. She and her husband have two children, both in school. Her position with SMTC has grown from part-time to full-time, supporting a small staff. Her psychotherapy practice is active and growing. She was honored by the Maine Women's Fund. She found time to help Dale McCormick's political campaign in 1996 and others in every election cycle, and she was appointed by Governor Angus King to the board of Jobs for Maine's Graduates.

The capacity to juggle all these roles is due in part to Lynn's personal credo. "I have never not worked, because not working doesn't feel right, and I hate not contributing to the family pot of money." It is also due to having a supportive husband who is good at parenting and whose full-time position has flexible hours He is also home evenings when Lynn has meetings. Her decision to run for office now is based on her children being still young enough to have fairly specific needs. Waiting until they are in their teens, when their demands become more complicated, might make running for and holding office much more difficult.

How did Lynn become who she is? Strong role models helped shape her belief that she could succeed in most anything she wanted to do. "My grandmothers were both incredible role models without knowing it or trying to be."

Lynn's maternal grandmother grew up on a farm in northern Vermont, married a farmer, and reared five children, including Lynn's mother. She also did all the other jobs that fell to a farm wife. It was a life of constant work, before electricity reached the countryside and everything was produced or grown on the farm. Early on, when Lynn's grandfather suffered a stroke, her grandmother said, "I knew things were going to hell in a handbasket. I knew we were headed for the poor farm, and if we were going there I wanted to run it." (Poor farms, an early effort by states to provide for indigent people, were maintained at public expense but were mostly run by their occupants under a local board of supervisors.) Seeing such a job advertised, Lynn's grandmother applied and was hired, then moved all her family to the farm, where they were ensconced in the family quarters. And run the farm is what her grandmother did. Tall and imposing, stern and comforting as required, she scheduled what needed to be done each day in the fields, letting her husband relay the orders, and ran everything else herself. She ordered supplies, oversaw the housekeeping and cooking, and dealt with the residents' medical problems. Lynn still wonders how her grandmother, who came from a relatively simple farm life, could hire people as required, work with the supervisory board, be the disciplinarian, and still be the person to go to when help was needed.

Lynn's paternal grandmother provides another story of survival and strength. Born into a well-to-do family in Burlington, she was stricken with polio at a young age. When the school system refused to let her attend classes, she took correspondence courses to become a bookkeeper, assuming that businesses would always need people with that skill. After marrying and giving birth to Lynn's father, she discovered that her husband was philandering, and she set out to create a life for herself. Upon finding a businessman she liked, she offered to work for him for a year with no pay, after which they would sit down and negotiate together how much she was worth. She was not only hired but went on to become president of the company.

Lynn attributes her strong work ethic to growing up with two strong role models and to her attempt to deal with two weak role models: her parents. Trying to please her father, who was inaccessible much of the time due to a drinking problem, led Lynn to work extra hard to please her employers. Coping with her mother's equally serious drinking problem, Lynn learned to take charge, fix supper, care for her mother, and locate her father and make sure he got a ride home—all early lessons in independence and coping.

Figuring out what she really wanted to do in life took Lynn some time. Trained as a teacher, she quickly realized that it no longer interested her. She drove a truck for a while, met another trucker, followed him to Maine, and married him. She started working as a clerk for a grocery chain, and in five years she became director of retail personnel. After her father's death, she found she no longer felt the need to work so hard to please. Her marriage came apart. The man she'd married as a rock to hold on to was no longer needed as a support. She took a job selling radio advertising and quickly became the top billing salesperson. When that job lost its glamour, she wanted to quit, but her boss told her to take a vacation and promptly loaned her $1,000.

Until then, Lynn had never traveled and never not worked. She says that she had always lived in the past—emulating her grandmothers—or for the future (to gain acceptance and approval). She had never lived in the present for its own sake. She went to Greece and traveled by herself, with no serious agenda. She met an old man who defined for her the pleasure of living in the moment. He told her, "In America you have tomatoes all year long. Here in Greece we only have them in the season, so that our enjoyment is therefore much greater."

In Greece, Lynn learned what she really wanted to do with her life. She was sitting in the amphitheater of a stadium historically important to Greek women and, as if on command, she walked down to the track area. Though not a runner, she found herself running all the way around until, raising her arms, she crossed some imaginary finish line. Although her career choice was not immediately clear, she realized that she "needed to do something with people, because I like being with people and it is something I do well."

After returning from Greece, Lynn entered Boston College School of Graduate Social Work, where she learned how to work with individuals and about social policy and economic equity. Her studies put names and faces on the issues with which she had life experiences. They gave her a more technical understanding of her own sense of social justice, showing her how individual struggles affect family struggles and how particular social policies affect lives.

She was happy in her single life, but, as she says, "Often when you are happy with yourself, you meet someone who is attracted to you." She did. They married and had a daughter—a birth that proved difficult, perhaps because she was thirty-eight at the time.

After finishing her mandatory two-year stint in community mental health, Lynn joined a group practice. Four years later she and her husband had a son. During this same period, she secured her position with SMTC and started serving on various boards to help write new legislation in the areas of her interests. Becoming involved with lobbying for various policies that concerned her, she began to realize that it would be better to have understanding people in the legislature rather than to attempt to influence the legislation. For this reason, she ran for office. It is this fervor that helped her win the nomination of her party and fires her hopes.

Lynn's credo is, "Tune into yourself and figure out what it is that your body, mind, and spirit want you to know. Develop your spiritual life—not necessarily church, although that may be the way for some—because when things get tough, and they will, you need a place to go. However you nurture your spirit—whether by fishing or praying or fluting, whatever is a nurturing, loving, spiritual presence—make that place larger in your life. You need to know where that place is and go there a lot."

Portland, Maine

*How many cares one loses
when one decides not to be
something but to be someone.*

— Coco (Gabrielle) Chanel

Achieving leadership using fairness and tact

BRENDA COMMANDER

Houlton, Maine   Born 1958
Elected chief of the Houlton Band of Maliseet Indians

" I hope that the tribe expands its services to the people, and that they get the legislation passed that will enable the tribe to determine its own destiny, not a path the state has set, but what the tribe wants to do, because they're the ones who know what the people need. It's going to take time—it can't happen overnight … I think I'll be around if they ever need or want me to help out."

It is difficult to comprehend the poverty in which Brenda was raised. At the age of two, weak with whooping cough, she was refused admittance to the local hospital because the family could not pay for her care. So her mother left her with her grandmother on Saint Mary's Reservation in Canada, where she was put in a hospital. After the grandmother's sudden death when Brenda was six, she returned to Houlton to live with her parents and nine siblings.

The third born, Brenda recalls being terribly shy in the Catholic school she attended, partly because her family was so poor and partly because she was Native American. Her parents and siblings struggled to survive by working together picking potatoes, working in the woods, helping farmers harvest their crops. In late summer the entire family would pick blueberries in the Machias area, where they lived in a tent on the barrens. Their house in Houlton had no water except what the children carried from a spring a quarter mile away. Donated clothes were often left on their doorstep. Before the winters ended and they were earning money again, Brenda's father—in order to make ends meet— would often have to sell the gun he'd used to put food on the table, only to have to buy another one in the fall.

79

When Brenda entered high school, she learned the joys of reading. She wrote stories and dreamed of becoming a writer, for which her mother sometimes chided her. Brenda viewed education as her way to escape Houlton. After graduating from high school, she applied for and received a two-year scholarship to Husson College in Bangor. She felt intimidated because all the other students were from well-to-do families. She took on two jobs, delivering food to the dorms and helping out in the school's financial aid office. After graduating she was taken in by a family of Micmacs and found a job with the Federal Housing Administration as a clerk in an on-the-job training program.

After Brenda married and became pregnant, she decided to return to Houlton, where she learned that the Maliseet band was attempting to organize to receive federal benefits as well as ride on the coattails of the Passamaquoddy and Penobscot tribes, who were then seeking federal recognition. She became the Maliseet's secretary for education, then in 1985 moved to the accounting department. Two years later, when the finance director left, Brenda took over the job, which she held for almost ten years. She is proud to hold these positions and be able to contribute to the tribe's improved welfare, not only as a member of the tribe but as a woman who has been charged with such responsibilities.

Brenda's husband died shortly after the birth of their daughter in 1985. This was just two months after her father's death from a massive heart attack. Brenda still struggles with the emotions surrounding these events. In 1992 she married a non–Native American who had a daughter from a prior marriage. Meanwhile, Brenda continued to manage the tribal finances.

When the Maliseet band's 1997 election rolled around, Brenda submitted her name to become the tribal chief; she was upset with how the current chief had allowed politics to roil the tribe, though she had avoided taking sides in the arguments until now. She won the election. Brenda helped introduce legislation to get state approval of the Maliseets as a tribal nation along with its own representative in Augusta. Although it did not gain sufficient support to be taken to a vote during the 2000 session, work continues to promote passage in the future. When Brenda's first term expired in 2001, she had gathered so much support as one of only three women chiefs of a Native American tribe in this country that she was reelected by a wide margin. She says her family life has suffered because she has devoted so much energy to tribal affairs. Yet she wants very much to continue. She does her job well, combining fairness and tact in working with her own people as well as many outside contacts.

Brenda wants to improve her knowledge of the tribal language. The Houlton band of Maliseets has secured a grant from the U.S. Department of Indian Affairs to support a teacher in the local school system to help maintain and continue their language, which has been stifled and almost eradicated by the church and government. Brenda hopes to attend at least some of the courses to hone her skills in her native language.

As for her spiritual beliefs, she has turned away from the Catholic religion in which she was raised. She says, "The attitudes of the church and of the government were to eliminate our culture as well as to take away our lands." Her beliefs are turning now toward those of her Indian forebears, who revered Mother Earth and valued protecting the land that supports them.

Houlton, Maine

Making the right choices

DONNA LORING

Richmond, Maine Born 1948

Law enforcement officer, represents the Penobscot Nation
in Augusta

hen Donna Loring was ten years old, her mother died after an epileptic seizure. Her father turned Donna and her brother over to his mother, and the children saw him only occasionally thereafter.

Forty years later, Donna's traumatic childhood and her father's abandonment are what she mentions first when talking about her life. An almost full-blooded Penobscot Indian, Donna was moved from Old Town to Indian Island into the house of a woman who was an ardent Baptist in a community that was 99 percent Catholic, the adopted religion of most Penobscot Indians. Her grandmother was the only one of her immediate family who was not a full-blooded Penobscot. Donna talks about going to church three times a week and twice more on Sundays. She was sent to public school in Old Town because her grandmother wouldn't hear of her attending the Catholic school on the island. Donna felt humiliated and alone in public school, isolated by the taunts of her peers because of her Indian heritage. She rebelled and, offering to pay for private school with money from her mother's Social Security, persuaded her grandmother to send her to Glen Cove Academy, a fundamentalist Christian school. Here she felt accepted and eventually graduated.

From these experiences emerged Donna's independent spirit, a degree of stubbornness, and a strong set of moral values. She describes herself now as "not Christian. I'm sort of a Heinz fifty-seven. I have a little bit of everything and I pick and choose … Going back to a school reunion thirty years later, I discovered I had a lot more in common with my classmates' basic values like honesty and truthfulness and integrity than I had realized ... even though I don't consider myself Christian, and they were very much Christian."

Despite her father's infrequent visits, Donna learned a lesson from one of his stories, although the lesson was in not repeating his actions. He had served with the 10th Mountain Division during World War II. When they were advancing up the Po River Valley in Italy, they encountered a company of German soldiers who signaled that they wanted to surrender. As they came down the opposite hillside, Donna's father noticed that the Germans were apparently concealing their weapons. He called out for everyone to hit the dirt. His action saved their lives, and they were able to overcome the enemy with little loss of life on their side. Later, Donna's father was offered a field promotion from corporal to second lieutenant—an offer he turned down because, as he explained to her, he didn't want the responsibility. Donna promised herself to never refuse responsibility.

In 1966, when the war in Vietnam was beginning to escalate, Donna volunteered for the army, in part because the head of her school wasn't going to recommend her for college. Although Donna had never been out of Maine, she knew that in order to advance in life, she couldn't stay on the island. She describes her twelve weeks of basic training as psychologically brutalizing, particularly for the women, a number of whom chose to flunk out and accept the associated penalties. She completed the course, joined the Signal Corps, and served in Vietnam, where her job was handling the casualty reports for the entire Southeast Asia command.

After her discharge in 1969, Donna moved around in a number of jobs before eventually coming back to Maine. She worked in a shoe factory for a few years before entering college, where she stayed until her money ran out. Then she alternated working and going to school until she graduated in 1986.

After college, Donna worked as a paralegal in the court system on Indian Island, as a reserve police officer, and then as a detective for the Penobscot County Sheriff's Department. It was here that she completed basic police training. She went from "acting corporal" to "acting sergeant," joking, "With all that 'acting' I should be put up for an academy award." She finally made police chief for the Penobscot Nation, a job she held for six years.

Donna's brother succumbed to alcoholism and drug abuse, eventually serving a prison term. She doesn't know why he went one way and she the other. He was murdered on Indian Island—the first murder there in more than eighty years. She suspects that his death was alcohol-related. The experience has left its scars, because they were close as children.

Following Donna's work as police chief, she was hired as head of security for Bowdoin College, the first woman to hold such a position. After six years she went to the University of Southern Maine as coordinator of Native American Studies. Now she works for the Penobscot Nation as a representative speaker with the title of Coordinator of Tribal State and International Relations.

Donna has a military bearing. Her upright, forceful gaze conveys her no-nonsense approach to life. "My belief is, we have choices in our life ... and we have to live with those choices ... It's not your mother or father or priest who makes them. You are the one who has to do that, and ... I want to be happy ... with the choices I've made."

State House, Augusta, Maine

Needing to become involved, learning people's needs

CHELLIE PINGREE

North Haven, Maine   Born 1954

*Farmer, founder of island business employing women,
state senator, running for the U.S. Senate*

" **I**f you'd told my parents when I was a rebellious teenager of thirteen, or if you'd told the people in this community when they
didn't want to have anything to do with me at first, that I would
someday wind up being the majority leader of the senate, or that I could
run for the U.S. Senate, they would have all said, 'You're crazy. You're
thinking of somebody else.' So if there's been a lesson in this for me, it's
that you don't have to have a perfect high school career, and you don't
have to go to law school, and you don't have to do everything right in
conventional terms to be able to push the envelope, or be successful, or
be respected for what you do."

There are few clues in Chellie Pingree's early life to indicate who
she is today. She grew up in Minneapolis and attended an experimental
high school in Minnesota based on the Outward Bound model. There she
met Charlie Pingree. She followed him to North Haven and never left.
She had intended to go to college but instead wound up living a back-to-
the-land existence on this Penobscot Bay island with a population of 350
people. She had moved from a state where almost everyone was an
immigrant to a place where many families had lived for generations.

She volunteered to help out in the island school, only to be told by
the superintendent that the school board had voted "that the girl who
drives the red pickup is never setting foot in our school." This was her
introduction to being an outsider in a community that was very protective of its sovereignty and didn't accept newcomers easily. "Everyone
knew who I was but not enough about me to trust me. It was a real blow.
What was I going to have to do to live here?"

Chellie decided that a degree in education would make it difficult for them to refuse her help in teaching. She attended the University of Southern Maine, then got her degree at the College of the Atlantic, in Bar Harbor. Along the way she married Charlie, who was studying boat-building, and they had a child. Chellie decided teaching was too difficult, but she really enjoyed plant science and growing things. When Charlie's grandmother left them a piece of land on North Haven, they started a small farm. Chellie raised chickens, kept a couple of cows, planted a large vegetable garden, and opened a farm stand. Delivering eggs to those who didn't want to come to the stand got Chellie invited into people's houses, where she sat at the kitchen table and learned their stories and more about the community.

Five years later, with three children, Chellie decided to open a store in town. Several local women put their knitted items in the store, and Chellie sold the yarn she had spun from her sheep. Soon the entire place was filled with locally made sweaters, hats, and other knitted items, plus skeins of yarn. After Chellie met a skilled knitting designer, thirty-five island women began sending their knitted products to New York and Boston every fall to be sold. The store started carrying kits based on her designer friend's work. Chellie started publishing a newsletter with her essays about living on an island. They caught people's fancy because it was a way of life they could imagine with nostalgic pleasure.

Wanting to become further involved in the community but afraid of being rejected again, Chellie decided to run for a job that no one else wanted—tax assessor. She won, and after a while ran for the planning board. She won again. Eventually she ran for the school board, "which was what I really wanted to do, because I had kids in school. I was interested in education, [which] tends to be the lightning rod of politics in a small town. I won and eventually became chair of the board."

During Chellie's twenty years on North Haven, she learned several lessons. Outsiders have to respect the sovereign bonds of the community and not try to make too many changes. "Given what was and is happening in a lot of coastal communities, the turmoil and so much of the land being sold to people 'from away,' I came to understand how important that was to people and realized that I probably had to get kicked around and pay my dues to show that I was here to be a valuable member." When she was expanding her yarn and sweater business, she decided to get a new desk—nothing fancy, just two filing cabinets with a door on top. "Oh, a new desk—who do we think we are?" asked one of the island women who worked for her. Thought Chellie, Oh my god, am I getting too big for my britches?

Twelve years after starting her business, Chellie was ready for something new. After hearing Colorado congresswoman Pat Schroeder speak one night, Chellie was approached by a woman who suggested Chellie should run for a senate seat that was being vacated by a woman. "I said, 'Oh yeah, right.' My daughter Hannah said, 'Mom, go for it.' All the way home I couldn't get it out of my mind. There was every reason not to; plus, I'd be going up against [a man] who had served in the house, run for Congress, and was well connected—everyone presumed it was his seat."

There used to be a saying in politics: A woman runs for office; a man stands for office. There's a certain sense of entitlement. The year was 1992. Chellie agreed to run, knowing it would be an uphill fight. "I'd really never done anything political outside of my community." She'd never even gone to a state committee meeting. To compensate, Chellie and her group of volunteers knocked on more than five thousand doors to get out her message that she cared about education, economic development for rural communities, and the environment. Mostly she talked about being a mom and a business owner and somebody with a different approach as well as being a fresh face.

She explains that part of her winning may have been due to the coincidence that it was the year that term limits were voted in. "There was a lot of 'throw the bums out' feeling or 'we've got to change something in politics.'" It was also what people were calling the "year of the woman." Chellie went on to become an effective legislator, not only being reelected three times but being so respected by her colleagues that she became majority leader of the senate until she was "termed out" and had to retire.

Chellie became enamored of politics. "Ever since I got elected, I realized that I absolutely love this work. Not to be corny, but there's a bit of a feeling of a calling. Even on days when it's horrible, I'm happy to go and do it. I enjoy the challenge."

Chellie believes that women bring to politics a lot of natural strengths, such as their ability at multitasking. "Men ... are encouraged to strive for what's ahead of them, and they are extremely linear in their thought patterns. Women ... think about ... balancing a lot of different things at the same time ... which is politics." Chellie thinks that the "unorderly process of democracy is part of its beauty. It allows a lot of different voices to play a role in what you're doing. Another strength is women's desire to bring consensus; they want everyone at the table feeling good when they finish up; they're not anxious to just get a settlement and get out of there. I think women bring a lot of compassion. They've got a lot of guts to take on the tough issues like abortion or gay rights or welfare reform in ways that come from their hearts."

Chellie's personal strength appears to be the understanding that you never win a fight without a struggle, and you have to make a few enemies or you never get anything done. "It's a tough lesson for a woman, because we want everyone to like us. But I come from a position of saying, 'Here are my values. Here's what I really care about.' If I couldn't bring that to the table, if something didn't feel right to me, it didn't matter who I was going to make angry or what the press was going to say. I have always felt that I know where my moral compass is. I've spent thirty years as part of a community where people don't mince their words. When people don't like what's going on here, they fight, they don't speak to each other. People are very blunt and honest. You get in a room full of fishermen, and there's no sweet-talking them out of anything."

The community of North Haven is what Chellie adopted and was adopted into. Even though now divorced from her husband, they see each other and he employs their younger daughter in his boatbuilding operation. When Chellie comes to the island to recharge her batteries, she is always amazed by how much she learns, particularly from her own children. It is where she launched her next campaign—running for the U.S. Senate in 2002 for the seat now held by Susan Collins.

North Haven, Maine

*Because of their age-long training in human relations—
for that is what feminine intuition really is—women
have a special contribution to make to any group
enterprise, and I feel it is up to them to contribute the
kind of awareness that relatively few men ...
have incorporated in their educations.*

— Margaret Mead

Helping women take better control of their lives

JANET C. McCAA

Cape Elizabeth, Maine   Born 1943
Collaborative attorney

" On one hand I'm a standard CEO—I want to make the rules, get it done, be very executive. If I were a man, I suspect ... I wouldn't be in touch with a lot of other pieces of myself that I'm forced to know because I'm a woman ... I learned to speak 'male' in law school and speak it relatively easily because the concepts have been my primary ones. I also speak 'female,' so I speak two languages ... My male colleagues only speak one but don't know they only speak one. This makes it easy for me to be a liaison, because I ... have a foot in both camps."

Three major and widely separated events have had a significant impact on Janet's life. The first was the death of her father; he was shot down over the Philippine Islands during World War II when she was an infant. Many years later, a lot of psychotherapy helped her learn to deal with feeling "reduced," as if she were less than a whole person.

The second event was another plane crash, when she was twenty-eight—almost exactly the same age as her father when he was killed. Janet, and only two other passengers out of twenty-eight, survived the crash. But more than 30 percent of Janet's body was burned, and she spent the next two and a half months in the hospital undergoing and recovering from reconstructive plastic surgery, followed by fifteen months of rehabilitation at home before she was ready to go back to her legal work in Washington. The experience made her aware that "life is a gift. I realized that I didn't have to be a lawyer or live in Washington. The

93

world was wide open. I could explore what my life had been and what I wanted it to be." Before the accident, Janet had lived "mostly intellectually." She now found this of little use. She began to explore her emotions, and in doing so came to realize that they had lain buried partly because allowing them to surface would have meant giving up control over her previously ordered life.

The third event came partly out of Janet's explorations of her emotions. Although not certain if she was a true Christian, Janet had joined the Episcopal Church while living in Washington and attended adult confirmation classes. On returning from the hospital, she was overwhelmed by the love shown her by members of the congregation. Although she still had many philosophical questions regarding the church, she was "anxious to explore my spiritual self and was intrigued by a world I couldn't see or touch. I started to examine the psychic world, through holographic practices, astrology, tarot cards, past life readings ... learning to trust my emotions instead of relying on intellect alone."

Several years after the crash, she was asked to sit on the Episcopal Diocese Ecclesiastical Court as one of two lawyers along with three priests. She would be the only woman. Several conservative priests had brought suit against another priest who had allowed one of the eleven "irregularly ordained" women priests from Philadelphia to conduct the Eucharist, thereby "disobeying the godly admonition of his bishop." This experience on the court changed her life. Not having thought of herself as a feminist before the trial, she certainly did afterward. She and the other lawyer found in favor of the defense; the priests found otherwise. The experience also made her decide to reject organized religion, along with many aspects of the application of law.

The combination of these events disconnected Janet from the "pillars" that had upheld her—family, church, and law. Out of the resulting chaos, she emerged with a strengthened determination to rethink her goals. She left the security of the National Labor Relations Board as a litigator and studied tax law at New York University School of Law, followed by five years of tax and business-related work in a Washington law firm. Then, following her instincts, at the age of forty-four she moved to Maine and joined a Portland law firm. Fourteen years later she and a partner co-founded their own firm, Johnson & McCaa, which celebrated its first anniversary in July 2002. Janet is beginning to think about the next phase of her life: developing legacy planning techniques focusing on issues of gender, money, power, and authority, and combining her organizational development skills with her general business law practice.

She says, "The walls we erect around ourselves are really only there as long as we are willing to have them there. When we want to push them back or push them away and expand the area inside, then it is relatively easy to do. I used to say 'the sky's the limit,' but why stop there? I want to be remembered for living ... fully and not taking no for an answer."

Portland, Maine

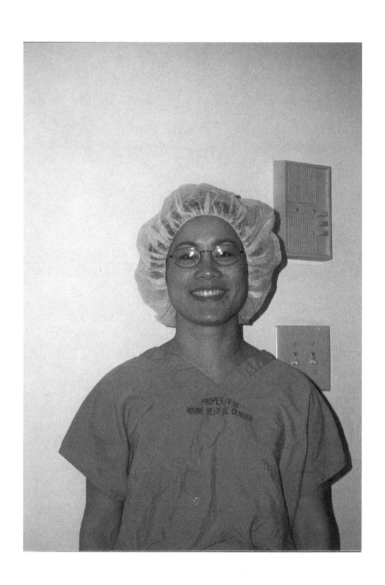

Soft as silk outside, steel determination inside

YUEER REN
(pronounced E R Ren)

Portland, Maine   Born 1959
Operating room nurse, single mom

" Always work toward having self-confidence. Make sure—trust yourself—you can do it. If you fail, it's not the end of the world. Keep upright. If at first you're not successful, as long as you believe, eventually it will come to you."

Yueer Ren was born in Ning Bo, China, one of five daughters in a middle-class family, and was raised in comfortable circumstances. Her father was a veterinarian; her mother worked at home. Both parents encouraged her to be herself and do her own thing. Her father was the typical authoritarian male figure, whom she found she shouldn't argue with but could go around. She finished high school, then studied at Hang Zhou University, all shortly after the cultural revolution that convulsed China.

Yueer married a year out of college and had a daughter, Jing Jing (known as J.J. in this country). By this time China had a policy of one child per family, so J.J. is an only child. Living under the same roof with her husband, daughter, mother, and a sister created a supportive environment that allowed Yueer to work full time at the university. Tiananmen Square and the repression that followed changed all that. Her world was suddenly turned upside down, and she felt it was time to leave China, if she could arrange it. Her husband supported her, even though they both knew that he and their daughter would be left behind, with little certainty that they would be allowed to join her. Through her work at the university and its cultural exchange program, she found

97

sponsors for study in America. One of these happened to be connected to the University of Southern Maine (USM). She had little knowledge of English but began studying it while waiting to leave China. She received her visa for the United States as a visiting scholar, and she came, leaving her comfortable family life behind.

Yueer arrived in Portland alone, making only a few friends who also spoke English. She was depressed and miserable, and she missed her daughter. She remembered seeing her for the last time, with her face pressed against the glass in the airport, bewildered at the thought of her mother leaving without her.

Yueer felt that she should study something practical in the United States. She chose nursing because it would give her an immediate means of supporting herself after graduation. She found that USM had a respected four-year nursing program and enrolled. She was accepted, although at first she hardly understood a word of the lectures. Her solution was to tape them, then in the quiet of her room at night she could look up all the words she didn't understand. At first, this meant going over each tape three or four times until she could understand and remember. She persevered and gradually the lessons came more easily, as did her English. By taking courses during the summer, Yueer managed to finish the program in three years—a remarkable feat.

As Yueer was getting ready to take her final exams, J.J., now nine years old, was allowed to join her mother. She was flown to Los Angeles, where Yueer met her, then quickly flew back to Maine for her exams. Yueer's husband was unable to gain permission to join them. After several years they agreed to divorce so both could go on with their lives. They remain friends, sharing concern for their daughter.

Yueer's experiences in Maine have made her believe in herself, her abilities, and her independence. She has been a full-time RN, for the past two years on operating room (OR) duty at Maine Medical Center. Recently she started working in the special care unit at the medical center. Her daughter, now enrolled at Haverford College, is completely fluent in English, with no trace of an accent. She also spent the spring semester of 2000 under scholarship at the Chewonki Foundation. Both mother and daughter have become naturalized U.S. citizens.

Yueer's story is a triumph of an individual's ability to surmount obstacles to achieve a goal. Yet this delicate-looking, very pretty woman has demonstrated that there is steel beneath her soft exterior. Perhaps you'll look for her one day at Maine Medical if you hear the address system call out, "E R to the OR."

Portland, Maine

Finding good in people

DIANE H. SCHETKY

Rockport, Maine   Born 1940

Forensic and clinical psychiatrist, writer,
educator, singer, artist

Diane's credo for herself is:

The highest good is like water.
Water gives life to the thousand things and does not strive.
It flows in places men reject and so is like the Tao.

Source: Lao Tsu
Tao Te Ching

As Diane Schetky speaks, you are instantly aware of her remarkable poise. You learn that she is quietly self-confident, has little need to talk about her accomplishments, appears totally comfortable in her own skin, and has found her own voice. "One of the beauties of aging is that I care less about what others think of me in terms of my appearance or views. I am more concerned with my integrity and remaining true to the values and beliefs that guide me. Aging is also a time of shedding, of ridding oneself of unnecessary baggage, possessions, or outdated modes of thinking."

Diane's feisty spirit and determination to be herself helped her overcome many obstacles, including an undiagnosed learning disability and several traumatic childhood events. She's now a successful forensic psychiatrist, who is often called upon to testify in court cases, and she has edited five books, co-authored another, and published more than thirty articles in professional journals.

101

Diane grew up in Greenwich, Connecticut, an affluent bedroom community outside of New York City. "It was the green ghetto, a community that was xenophobic, homophobic, and very class-oriented. A WASPy family where all the women went to Vassar and all the men went to Yale, and heaven help you if you didn't fit that mold."

Traumas came early. She spent months in bed with typhoid fever, then at age ten she was informed that her father was leaving home. She learned only later that he'd had an affair with a movie actress and even later that they had a child. Her parents divorced, then each remarried. Although she lived with her mother, she was never comfortable with that arrangement; her mother constantly tried to mold her into a life that was repugnant to her. She was also forced to deal with suicide: the deaths of the mothers of two childhood friends, one of whom killed her three children as she took her own life. Diane doesn't dismiss the possibility that these events contributed to her later interest in medicine, then in mental illness.

Diane's relationship with her mother was always difficult. In addition she saw little of her father while she was growing up because of his work and travel. Then, after her parents split, she saw him even more rarely until much later—after she broke with her mother. This break was not only over the difference between their views of what was important, but because Diane's mother attempted to turn her away from her father. Later, Diane and her father began to see each other more frequently and he became a male role model. At six feet five inches, he is literally and figuratively a giant of a man. He became the publisher of *Life* magazine and later chairman of Time, Inc. After retirement he became Chairman of the New York Public Library and helped restore some of its former glory. Later still he became Chairman of the American Academy in Rome, finally retiring for good at age eighty-five. Diane says, "I admire his intellect, love of life, perseverance, modesty, and the quiet way in which he gets things done. He puts his weight behind admirable humanitarian causes and in giving of himself receives much satisfaction."

Diane describes her performance in school as "less than stellar. I was an occasional troublemaker, who didn't pay attention in class, becoming known as Dizzy Dinny. Poor grades led to my enrollment in every private school in Greenwich, with little improvement. I was finally sent to boarding school, and I was glad to be out of my home situation, which was becoming untenable." Because her grades weren't good enough to get her into any of the "Seven Sister" schools, Diane wound up at Connecticut College, which she disliked because it was "anti-intellectual." Here she found her first incentive—to buckle down and get out of there. In two years she made the dean's list and was able to transfer to Sarah Lawrence College, where she says, "I really came alive and started developing some self-confidence."

Because Diane never did well on exams, part of her success at Sarah Lawrence may have been due to the school's emphasis on class participation. Although Diane graduated with a bachelor's degree with a concentration in studio art, she had realized early that her artistic talent was limited. So she pursued her interest in medicine as well, taking all the courses necessary to qualify for medical school.

Partly because of being female, and partly because of her humanities background, Diane had difficulty being accepted for medical school, despite having fulfilled all the course requirements. She says, "At that time in the early sixties few women were being accepted—if you were pretty, the odds were that you would soon leave the field to have babies. If you weren't, the other students would complain." But ultimately she was accepted at Case Western Reserve University, School of Medicine. As she says, "Hard work and perseverance got me through, and I thrived on the clinical work which was introduced early. Frequent nights on call during my training, in their own perverse way, enhanced my ability to make judgment calls on my own."

Diane married a fellow student while still in medical school. "It was for love, plus the security of being married to a man who was two years ahead of me." After a year in pediatrics—"I realized I needed more or less normal sleep to survive"—she switched to psychiatry, which was also her husband's field. During this period they had their first child, a boy. With no provision in those days for maternity leave, she returned to work after having taken her vacation time, then was allowed to work part time. Later the couple had a second boy. After completing her training in adult and child psychiatry, Diane directed a child psychiatry clinic on a part-time basis. Then, after thirteen years of marriage, it became obvious to her that the only interest the couple shared was the children and medicine. Diane left, feeling guilty about taking the boys away from their father, but knowing she had to do it if she was to feel true to herself.

She married on the rebound, taking up a sophisticated corporate-wife lifestyle back in Connecticut. She describes her second husband as urbane and intellectually stimulating but unable to warm up to the role of stepfather, so she did most of the parenting while attempting to start a private psychiatric practice. The marriage ended, and she moved to Rockport, Maine, in 1986.

She started a practice in psychiatry in her home office. She married again, this time choosing someone with whom she could spend her retirement years. They did well while vacationing at sea but not so well on land, each having had some expectation that they could change the other. Diane soon realized her mistake and again divorced. "Having a career and my own strong identity has made it easy, perhaps too easy, to slide in and out of marriages. I no longer feel the need to be married and am quite content with my own company and the freedom to pursue my many interests. I enjoy the company of male friends, but also cherish my autonomy and solitude."

Diane's practice in psychiatry has long included children and adolescents who were victims of sexual abuse. She wrote her first article on the subject of incest. Few psychiatrists were dealing with incest at the time, so she received many referrals and was called to testify in court cases. "Nobody taught child forensic psychiatry back then, so I learned from judges, attorneys, and my own mistakes. She co-edited a book entitled *Child Psychiatry and the Law*. The first of its kind, it became a seminal book for teaching in the field. In addition to seeing abused children in her private practice, she started teaching in this field at Maine Medical Center, in Portland.

It wasn't long after Diane moved to Rockport that she became involved in the criminal side of forensic psychiatry by working in the Maine State Prison, in Thomaston, and Downeast Correctional, near Machiasport. Her involvement began by helping out a colleague who was going on leave, but she became fascinated—learning about herself in the process, as well as learning to see the good in people no matter what they've done. Her interest led to work at the Northern Maine Youth Detention Center as staff psychiatrist. Although she was largely self-taught due to the lack of facilities in Maine for doing a fellowship, she was eventually able to take—and pass—the forensic board exams.

Diane recently decided to give up her private practice in order to concentrate on forensic psychiatry. One of the reasons for this decision was the lack of time allowed under managed care to do a proper job in either evaluation or therapy. She finds forensic psychiatry intellectually challenging and a continual test of her integrity to speak the truth as she sees it. Testifying in court has enhanced her ability to think on her feet.

She occasionally finds herself taking unpopular positions—testifying against physicians in malpractice suits involving alleged boundary violations, or defending persons accused (falsely) of molesting children.

Diane has also recently been appointed clinical professor of psychiatry at the University of Vermont School of Medicine at Maine Medical Center. She writes a bimonthly column on ethics for a professional journal. She is starting a prison hospice program at Maine State Prison, training inmates to be hospice volunteers. She has always loved music, sings with the Down East Singers, and—with the Surry Opera Company—learned an opera in the Georgian language and performed it in Tbilisi in conjunction with the Georgian State Opera Company. Playing the piano gives her much pleasure and is a source of relaxation. Painting, drawing, and travel do the same.

One of Diane's early role models in literature was Piper's *The Little Engine That Could*. Imagine a little girl as a steam engine who puffs and chugs trying to pull a heavy load up the mountain: I think I can, I think I can … I thought I could, I thought I could.

She did!

Rockport, Maine

Combining hard work and quiet persistence

JOAN YEATON

Addison, Maine   Born 1941

Llama farmer, director of facility for the chronically
mentally ill, B&B owner

Joan Yeaton appears totally at ease juggling three businesses. It is
only the intensity of her responses that hints at her involvement in
multiple commitments. That, and the fifty-some llamas grazing in
the field outside, and the frequent phone calls for her bed-and-breakfast
business, as well as requests to discuss issues about the chronically mentally ill at the facility she directs. In addition, she and her husband have
six grown children and care for her elderly father-in-law, who lives in a
separate apartment that she and her husband added on to their home.

Joan's major responsibility is directing a facility in Milbridge that
cares for the chronically mentally disturbed who have difficulty managing their own affairs but no longer need full-time institutional care.
Some reside in the facility; some come only for help on a day-by-day
basis. Joan has done this for more than four years—trying to hold on to
staff despite low wages, pleading with the legislature and the bureaucra-
cy for more resources, and dealing with the many problems that arise
with her charges, such as arranging an out-of-state abortion for a young
woman who was incapable of caring for a baby—which also involved
finding someone willing to provide funding for everything, including
transportation and housing. Prior to her position at this facility, Joan
spent eight years working with the deaf and blind in Maine. "I mean
they were both deaf and blind," she emphasizes.

It is the llama farm that provides Joan the tranquility she needs to
offset the strains of her main job. But even this is a story of hard work
and many years of effort.

Before moving to Maine, Joan lived in Exeter, New Hampshire, where she ran a real estate business for sixteen years. In the midst of that she divorced the father of her three children and later married her current husband, Lee—who owned an insurance agency—which added three more children to her household. As the children began to leave the nest and go off to school, Lee asked Joan what she would like to do next. She recounts that conversation: "I thought we could do most anything; we could even buy a couple of llamas. That was just off the top of my head and not necessarily serious. But for Christmas, this llama arrived! And he was very lonely and we had to get another llama. Then we found coming home from work that we just liked the farming life."

Thus began a major transformation in their lifestyle. Lee came home from his office one day and said he really didn't like the insurance business anymore. Always a risk taker, Joan decided that "we could sell everything we owned: our houses, our businesses, everything. And come up to Maine where we would farm and start a new business together. And we did it. This was a real labor of love. We lived first in a little mobile home where the garden is now. We cleared enough land to see the water, and we just started chipping away at all that needed to be done."

For Joan, buying a hundred-acre site overlooking Pleasant Bay in Addison was not entirely impetuous. She was born in nearby Machiasport and lived there for several years before moving to Massachusetts, where her father had been transferred. For a couple in their mid-forties, to homestead an uncleared piece of land was no easy job. They cut the trees as close to the ground as possible, let the grass come up, then limed and fertilized; plus each year they bush-hogged to deter new tree growth—a technique that helps avoid the erosion caused by uprooting. Time did the rest, gradually rotting the stumps until there are now fields for pasture. During this period the number of llamas grew to fifty, and they provide some income from the sale of wool and young animals.

Joan's love for llamas began in South America, where she spent time just after college and married her first husband. She is quick to talk about her llamas, each of whom she calls by name—how intelligent they are (their brain is two-thirds larger than that of a horse although their body size is two-thirds smaller), how shy they are, how they walk up and kiss you after they get to know you, how agile they are, and how their main weapon against predators is spitting in their face.

Having a llama farm meant that Joan and Lee had to build a barn and erect fences. After the land was cleared, they also built a house—big enough for their six children to come and visit. Having a house that big meant finding a use for it on a more continual basis—hence the *Pleasant Bay Bed and Breakfast*. People come at all times of the year, walk, take in the view, explore the surrounding land, and commune with the llamas. It is a successful venture, regarded fondly by many who stay there.

What caused Joan to become such a risk taker? The seeds were planted by her grandmother, who was married for many years to a fundamentalist minister in Boston who spent much of his life searching for and rooting out perceived evil. He ruled his household autocratically. In spite of that, Joan's grandmother raised seven children—all of whom looked to her—and still "did her own thing" while being subservient to her husband when he was around. "When he wasn't around," Joan said, "she just let loose. I'm not sure how she managed, but she did." After her grandfather died, her grandmother moved in with Joan's family. It became a true matriarchy, a household run by women—mother, grand-mother, and three daughters. Although Joan's father also lived there, he seemed happy to let the women run it, negotiating between his own mother and his wife.

If Joan's grandmother planted the seeds of independence, they were nurtured by her mother, whose husband died early. She raised Joan and her sisters by herself. "I sort of broke out of that small town mold of just doing what was expected of me pretty early," says Joan. She wanted to see the world, because she had grown up in such a small town. Although she wanted to attend college on the West Coast, she won a scholarship to the University of Montana in Bozeman—way out in the country in those days. She loved it and she loved being on her own. She decided not to pursue the nursing program she had enrolled in but instead focused on teaching. After college, she started teaching immediately, went to South America, married soon after, and spent some time traveling and moving around. The marriage didn't work, but by this time she had three children and was living in Exeter, New Hampshire, where she divorced her husband. After several years on her own and with her real estate business, she met Lee.

If Joan's abilities and energy are clearly apparent, what isn't so immediately obvious is her quiet persistence. If she doesn't gain her objective directly, she goes at it in different ways until she achieves her goal—or wears down the opposition. It is this characteristic that makes her an effective administrator, particularly in an agency strapped for support and staff. But this same ability has sustained her other achievements, and the llamas and B&B guests are grateful for that.

Addison, Maine

Dreams are necessary to life.

— Anais Nin

Reinventing herself several times

SUSAN STONESTREET

Lincolnville, Maine   Born 1948
Ordained minister and parish pastor

" I would say to follow your heart but do it responsibly; do it with passion, but don't do it without thinking. [When I was younger] I thought a lot, knew the good things that I should do, but didn't know anything about following my heart and didn't discover it truly until I went into the ministry. I thought that I had been happy doing what I had been doing the first half of my life, but realize now ... I wasn't doing what 'makes my heart sing,' and now I am. There needs to be a balance in life between passion, heart, and mind."

This is Susan Stonestreet's story of change and growth. It is the story of an unusually independent woman who isn't afraid to speak her mind, who is direct yet approachable, and who is sincere and compassionate. Perhaps because of the lateness of her entrance into the ministry, it is a story still fresh with the excitement of discovery.

Religion was not part of Susan's youth in Washington, D.C. Occasionally her family would attend church, but after three Sunday school sessions, Susan flatly refused to go again. Looking back on those years now, she says, "My mother was God for me ... a compassionate, loving, caring woman. And she remained so for all the years of her life." Susan describes her father as a "good man," who always worked hard in the store he managed and loved, but who had a hard life growing up, didn't often participate in family activities, and was unable to express his feelings.

Susan attended Miami University in Ohio about the time of the Kent State killings by National Guardsmen. The shooting of those Ohio college students/anti-war demonstrators still reverberates in her memory.

113

Susan married at the end of her senior year in college. "We basically had nothing in common, but I was twenty-one. I didn't know who I was—I didn't know what I was supposed to be doing. My parents never pressured me [to get married]; it was just sort of what you were expected to do." Susan ended the marriage when her husband ordered her around one too many times. "I said okay, but my next thought was, never again will someone … tell me what to do. That was the beginning of my independence." She went to court to change her name and chose "Stonestreet," that of a female ancestor whom she admired. It was her first reinvention.

Susan's undergraduate degree in American Studies didn't qualify her for a useful job, but she became interested in crisis counseling, was accepted back at Miami University for a two-year program to obtain her master's degree, and while there worked at the crisis intervention center. Four years later, thinking she might get her doctorate in the field, she interviewed at the University of Florida in Tallahassee.

While in Florida, Susan reinvented herself again. During her visit she saw a newspaper ad for an administrative assistant to the president of a small brokerage firm in Sarasota. "I don't know what possessed me, but I decided to talk to them about it." She was hired, and she left her position at the crisis intervention center in Ohio.

Susan obtained her brokerage license but realized that she'd never be more than an assistant at the small firm. So she became a financial planner with American Express, and stayed on for fifteen years. An older brother joined her in what became a lucrative practice.

Her transition to the ministry had many components. During visits to shut-ins in Florida, she became close to a deeply religious elderly woman who had moved to Florida from Camden, Maine. Susan knew Maine from numerous visits. But what made her aware that she should be doing something more fulfilling than financial planning came when a doctor client told her, "Susan, you've made too much money for me this past year. Now I have to pay more taxes. What are you going to do about it?" She says now, "I could have told him I knew of several very good charities who would love to help him with his problem, but I was too shocked to say so." On a trip to Maine shortly after, she picked up a Bangor Theological Seminary catalog. "Sitting outside in my rented car, I read it, and with tears streaming from my eyes I said out loud, 'You know this is what you want to do.'"

She returned to Florida and told her brother she was going to quit the firm and go to seminary. He said, "What are you talking about?

You've never even been to church!" Susan's response was, "I don't know [why], but I'm going to do this." She applied, was accepted, and entered seminary in the fall of 1995—reinventing herself once again. As she says, "I lived most of the first half of my life wanting nothing to do with the church. I had tried to live my life by the Golden Rule, not even knowing that it was from the Bible and from Buddha ... just that it was a good way to treat people."

Perhaps because Susan did not have a Christian background, her seminary experience produced a theological perspective not customary for most. "I did not hear the words 'sin' and 'cross' or 'suffering' and 'salvation' on any regular basis [growing up]. I entered seminary with a clean slate ... My theology is grounded in the teachings of Jesus ... I understand that Good Friday had to take place but am uncomfortable placing my acceptance of Christianity only on Jesus' final sacrifice. My theology is simply not sacrificial. It is reverent and full of thanksgiving that Jesus lived, died, and lives on for me and for all who care to hear his words.

"A theology based only on Christ's suffering is not full enough for me. I believe it often leads to feelings of guilt and self-hate [and] can lead to never feeling good enough. A theology of thanksgiving is life- giving and helps me remember what I am thankful for and what I continue to strive for. I believe we are called to ... treat one another with compassion as Jesus treated those he touched during his life ... to show one another through Christ-like actions what it means to know God's love in a world filled with ... violence, hatred, suffering, and intolerance."

Susan graduated from the Seminary and was ordained in the United Church of Christ (Congregational Church) in 1999; she now has a parish in Lincolnville. Part of her excitement about the ministry is in reaching beyond Christianity to explore the teachings of other religions, as well as the many layers of meaning in parables from the Bible. "I see my role as being a compassionate, spiritual friend for whoever chooses to experience God's presence in their lives. Some of my clergy colleagues say to me, "Susan, you're very innocent and naive," and I say, "Yes, and isn't that wonderful."

Camden, Maine

115

*"Love, beauty, and the underlying harmony of the universe:
these are the truths in my heart."*

LINDA THOMPSON

Cape Split, Addison, Maine   Born 1940

Universalist, religion student, linguist, musician, sternman

T he *Osprey* turns into the wind and slows. The captain grabs the
toggle and hauls the pot. With the trap on board and open, the
captain starts sorting, discarding those lobsters below legal size,
banding the keepers and placing them in the holding tank. Meanwhile
the sternman empties the bait pocket, throws the old bait overboard,
puts a freshly baited pocket in the trap, then cleans out any remaining
catch—such as crabs and urchins—and closes it. As the boat accelerates,
moving to its next destination, she shoves the trap off the washboard,
leaving a swarm of noisy gulls to pick over the remains on the water.

Linda Thompson is not someone you would expect to be a sternman
on a Down East lobster boat. She is sixty, lithe of body, and "from
away"—having moved to Maine from Burlington, Vermont, a decade ago
to marry Billy Thompson. But neither is Billy your normal lobsterman,
although he has lived and lobstered off Cape Split for fifty years. Nor is
the *Osprey* owned and operated in the usual manner.

Giving up a high-paying position in Burlington in charge of external
affairs for a statewide agency—as well as many friends and activities,
and two grown children still living there—to move to Maine was a
radical choice for Linda. Then fifty-one, she had spent a more than a
quarter-century in Vermont. "I changed everything in my life in one fell
swoop: marital status, parental status, job, house, environment. Some
brave instinct led me to the realization that there was more to life than
all I had. Though it is a desire seldom acknowledged in today's culture, I
yearned to share my days with someone I loved. I was exhilarated to be

taking this step as an adult, in perfect freedom, committed to making all the adjustments involved."

Linda's move doesn't seem nearly as dauntless as it actually was until you learn that she has an intellectual bent with degrees in religion and French. Her religious view encompasses the vast variety of cultures in the world—with all their manifestations of the holy—rather than the more limited Judeo-Christian belief in a single, all-powerful being.

Linda loves music and plays the flute and piano as often as she can. She is an avid admirer of French culture and speaks the language fluently. At one time she worked for Rossignol, the French sports company, becoming import/export manager of their tennis division. She has also worked at the University of Vermont to coordinate their art programs, and was in charge of external relations—working with the Vermont legislature—for a not-for-profit state agency. "The trajectory has not been one I have carefully controlled, organized, or preconceived. It is marvelous to me that life happens, and is embraced, and that possibility continues to unfold. Choice, for me, is the full use of one's gifts, the recognition of opportunities, taking notice, giving expression, contributing, turning, loving, and moving forward into one's destiny."

At least two major threads run though Linda's life. One is a passionate adherence to freedom—freedom to make her own choices. "In my childhood, my father attempted to make all my choices for me. My feisty young spirit had to carve out a resilient zone of internal liberty. My independence came from my thoughts and feelings, which were beyond violation."

Music was an important part of her growing up. She was expected to study piano, like her sisters, but chose the flute instead. She was sent to "a thoroughly obnoxious summer camp where I would have the dubious privilege of meeting the right young ladies." Despite her research into other schools that she believed would be better suited to her talents and interests, she was sent to a boarding school that she dubs the "nunnery." She was informed she would go to one of two colleges; her own thoughts were unexplored, not to mention ignored. The only way she could exert her wishes was to choose the college that her sisters had not chosen.

Linda's first departure from the track that had been chosen for her was to marry at the end of her sophomore year. With her husband, a young college history professor, she moved to Burlington—where he was teaching—and transferred to the University of Vermont. During the spring of her junior year, she had a daughter, an experience she calls "the most ecstatic of my life." After this she was surprised to find that her studies became more enjoyable, and she started taking them more seriously. Several years and two more children later, she completed her degree in comparative religion and obtained a master's degree in French. Spending long periods in France with her husband, she developed a passion for all things French.

Although many years of Linda's first marriage were happy, she became increasingly aware that she had more growing to do. Even her husband recognized that she should continue with her studies. When she suggested studying for her Ph.D. at McGill University, he informed her that it wasn't practical. Thus began a rift that culminated during one of their trips to France where they were due to spend many months. When this discord became obvious, Linda returned home with the children to start working for Rossignol.

Linda's fascination with religion and spirituality—the other important thread running through her life—has been with her since childhood, when she sat on top of a mountain and was struck with a reality in which all things sang in harmony beyond description. The experience changed her life. Her subsequent study of religion, her intellect, her life experiences, and this early vision of the harmony of all things led Linda to formulate these coherent beliefs:

"I do not believe that an omniscient deity closely fashioned after humans is in charge of the universe. A God so referential, so mechanical, so dangling at the end of a statement of faith, is all wrong in my heart. There is no word for the ineffable beauty of the inner spirit of things … The word 'God' points to an entity far too small and paltry to deserve my praise. The all-encompassing being, the spirit of the universe, is expansive beyond any human understanding. This spirit has no form, for there is no correspondence between the categories of our discursive minds and the mystery of the universe.

"I do not take the historical figure Jesus Christ to be the once-only eruption of the divine into history, but the recognition that it is we ourselves who are holy. Salvation is in the present, 'at hand,' because it is ever available. The 'Kingdom of God' is within you and the divine child is a universal archetype—the Christ Child sharing his divinity with the divine child of other cultures. It seems to me that the growing awareness of the wonderful variety of cultures in our world . . . makes it increasingly difficult for Christians to adhere to a claim of exclusivity. I believe that

119

Christ is an eternal reality, predating and postdating Jesus of Nazareth, who is one manifestation of that wider reality.

"I do not subscribe to a notion that absolute truth has been set down by 'God' in a specific book, written over centuries by humans with a wide variety of motivations. It is both parochial and arrogant to assume that 'God' is speaking or acting on behalf of one group of humans at the expense of others. The Bible is full of this kind of apparent nonsense which may have rendered the world comprehensible at the time of writing. No one written word on the human soul is exclusively sacred. Rather the written word, art, music, and dance become sacred whenever form embodies content in such a way that the soul of the beholder is uplifted ... What is more wondrous than the apprehension of beauty? Love, beauty, and the underlying harmony of the universe: these are the truths in my heart. What a joyful turning it would be if we listened to, and lived by, the underlying harmony."

Linda's husband, Billy, descends from the Wass family, the earliest settlers of Cape Split. His mother was Susie Wass Thompson, an accomplished amateur artist with works in a number of prominent collections, including the Farnsworth Art Museum. When Linda met Billy, he had been divorced by his wife, the granddaughter of the internationally known artist John Marin, and had two young children to raise, the great-grandchildren of the artist. Billy had served in the Air Force, then for a number of years had stopped fishing full-time to run a small earth-moving construction company. But he had become disheartened by the trend to destroy older houses for development rather than restoring them. Linda says, "Despite being as far removed from the world of my background as anyone could be, there was something mysteriously similar about us, and we felt at once that we had always known each other."

When they married, Linda found that there were no suitable jobs in that remote corner of Maine. So they decided to fish together for lobster. This meant a new boat; the old wooden Beal's Island craft that Billy owned was no longer serviceable. They built the *Osprey*, each contributing half and being co-captains. But Linda, realizing that Billy knew things from long experience that she might never learn, soon decided that real equality meant doing what each did best. Billy now runs the boat, and she is the sternman.

The depth of Linda's involvement with religious matters came to the fore after she moved to Maine. Initially she worked on a second master's degree at the Bangor Theological Seminary. But marriage, the care of her two stepchildren, and the length of the commute caused her to relinquish this after two years. More recently, Linda joined the board of the Maine Sea Coast Mission Society, which operates a boat to deliver services of several kinds to Maine's inhabited islands. After three years the board asked her to become vice president. She refused—due to the length of the commute to its headquarters in Bar Harbor, the amount of time that the position required, and the presumption that the position could lead to being the organization's president. She has also been instrumental in converting a small, unused schoolhouse on Cape Split into a chapel and helping to arrange a wide variety of services there during the summer months.

Linda's life in Maine has been both rewarding and fulfilling. Perhaps her biggest challenge as well as her best reward is in helping to raise and motivate her two stepchildren, who are a generation removed from her biological children. In addition, her Bangor studies led to friendship with a New Testament and Greek scholar, who has been urging her to write, rather than take more courses in theology. She says, "I haven't completely fulfilled that call—I did give one sermon up at the chapel on the 'Kingdom of God'—but then I haven't completed everything I'm on earth to do."

Addison, Maine

"Wicked" independent

LINDA ALVERSON

Oxbow, Maine   Born 1948
Forestry and wildlife biology consultant

Linda Alverson has had to become a real force, not only to cope with the harsh environment of the northern Maine forest where she works, but to overcome the reluctance of men to have a woman work alone in the woods. This was especially true more than twenty years ago when she started. The forestlands of just one of her clients, the Seven Islands Land Company, cover a million acres (more area than the entire state of Rhode Island), where she is documenting wildlife habitat across all the company's holdings. Some of her other clients include the U.S. Fish and Wildlife Service, Maine Inland Fisheries & Wildlife, The Nature Conservancy, and the Maine Audubon Society.

Linda makes her home—comfortable, but still a work in progress—in Oxbow, population sixty-nine. The closest shopping area to this beautiful, remote region north of Baxter State Park is forty miles away in Presque Isle. Linda describes her marriage to George McPherson two years ago, in which she gained two stepdaughters and five grandchildren, as perhaps the happiest time of her life. Having no children of her own, she particularly appreciates the chance to develop close relationships with her grandchildren.

She also loves the forest. She is a natural bridge between industry and conservationists because of her knowledge and love of wildlife as well as her passion for maintaining the biodiversity that is essential for the long-term health of both the forest and its wildlife. Her dream is to manage a 5,000-acre section of forest where she can practice biodiversity in forest management and still make a reasonable profit for the landowner. "There are a lot of people who think you can't do both, but

123

there has to be a way; otherwise we're going to destroy the forests." This has become Linda's clarion call to all who will listen.

Snippets from Linda's work reveal what she's about. When, working for Diamond International early in her career, she was informed that she couldn't go out on a snowmobile by herself, she told them, "Well, you better make that the rule for everybody in this company, not just the women." At Seven Islands, the senior forester would call Linda on the radio if she wasn't in by four in the afternoon to see if she was okay, something he never did for the men. After a number of such incidents, she told him on the phone, "Okay, Dad, I've had enough of this. I'm on my way in." He never did it again. More recently, she was sleeping near her pickup when she woke to the sound of a moose chomping on vegetation right next to her tent. Knowing that her tent was less than three feet high, and the moose could easily step on her in the dark, she sat up and said, "Hey, get out of here!" The moose went running off into the woods. Perhaps it's incidents such as these that have caused some to say, "She's wicked independent."

Although Linda hasn't experienced out-and-out harassment in her work, she believes that there is a glass ceiling for women working in the forest. She has been employed directly by three different companies, none of which has women in senior positions; each time she has taken a new job, she has had to prove herself all over again. On one job in which she had a road laid out and was about to flag it on the ground, the senior forester asked if she knew how to use a compass. "I was really pissed that he'd asked that kind of question. If you're a trained forester, you obviously know how ... But you have to learn how to treat it lightly. So I just punched him on the arm and said, 'Of course I do.'"

How did Linda become such a forthright, independent woman? One clue may come from her relationship with her father. Linda was (and still is) close to her father while she was growing up in New York State, where he was a teacher. (Her mother was a nurse.) Perhaps Linda heeded the stories her father told about one of his forebears, a superintendent of schools in Syracuse. In a battle over whether the district would spend money on a vocational school or a gym, when it decided on a gym, he retired on the spot. Linda seems like a chip off the old block. An important mentor for her was a biology professor at Nazarene College, outside of Boston, which Linda attended in the middle of the peace movement during the 1960s. She says, "He was a horrible lecturer, but I loved working for him, which I did every summer through college." The field biology course she took from him in the Adirondack Mountains opened up the outdoor world for her.

Linda, who at five feet nine inches played basketball throughout her college career, went back to school at the University of Maine at Orono to make up for the time she had spent participating in sports instead of studying. Then she pursued a master's degree in forestry, focusing on "remote sensing" (using aerial mapping and other indirect methods). She wrote her thesis, although when her advisor told her he thought she needed forty pages of literature review that she didn't think were necessary to prove her conclusions, they parted ways. As she says, "I have the knowledge, so the piece of paper wasn't necessary."

Aside from her work and family, Linda does mentoring—Girl Scouts and students from the Camp Kieve Science Camp in Nobleboro. She carries her enthusiasm for her work with her when she volunteers to talk to students at high schools on career day, although she gets discouraged: "So many won't go that extra mile—say, for instance, to become a doctor instead of a physical therapist." She believes that young women can do anything if they are willing to work for it, and she hopes that some of her own enthusiasm about her career rubs off on those around her.

Oxbow, Maine

Comfortable with herself

ANN GIBBS

Vienna, Maine   Born 1959
Maine state horticulturist

Some children are lucky enough to grow up in a household where both parents are role models, where each supports the other, and where gender roles aren't an issue. Such was the case for Ann Gibbs. Her father was a veterinarian who spent most of his time teaching. Her mother helped her husband get his degree, then as soon as the children were born went back to get her Ph.D. in entomology, specializing in aquatic insects. This meant that, as often as not, her father changed diapers and helped with the cooking and cleaning. Ann often accompanied her mother on field trips. It was a comfortable life, says Ann, the second of four children and the only female child. The family did many things together—including hiking and camping—which Ann says was really important.

Most of Ann's early life was spent in a town near Montreal. Much of her schooling was in Canada, until junior high school when her family moved to Maine. Her mother became the first woman to teach life sciences at the University of Maine at Orono. By this time Ann was back in Canada studying for her undergraduate degree in horticulture at the University of Guelph, the agricultural affiliate of the University of Toronto. In this endeavor, she received a great deal of encouragement from her mother. After a few years in various jobs, Ann decided to pursue a graduate program in historic landscape in Connecticut. She found that she loved it too much to make it a career rather than an avocation, so she returned to Maine to get a graduate degree in plant physiology.

During this time, Ann met a man who eventually became her husband. "We lived together for twelve years ... Being married wasn't an

127

issue until we decided we wanted to have a family and my father ... thought it would be a good idea if we got married. So we [did], but it never changed our relationship or our commitment. It was just ... a formality." Ann says having a child was "the best thing we've ever been through," although she was scared to do so, wondering whether they should add any more to the population of the earth. But she says that having a son, now five, is "really special, and it works for both of us since we know each other so well."

Ann was appointed state horticulturist for the Maine Department of Agriculture well before their son was born. She is the first woman to hold the job since it was established around 1910. The position deals primarily with regulating plant pests to make sure that only healthy plants are sold in the state or are moved out of state. A secondary role is to act as an information center to help people who call with plant problems. Her staff also acts as a liaison with the U.S. Department of Agriculture on plant health issues. She has held the post for more than ten years with a small staff to do inspections and assist with solving plant problems.

The problems associated with being a woman in Ann's profession seem to roll right off her, either unnoticed or dismissed. Yes, she's had people who insist on talking "to the man in charge." She simply ignores them and keeps on talking.

Ann's speech is as self-assured as her demeanor. Her walk and build are that of a runner, and she looks younger than her forty-one years. She knows how to relax and wants to be able to take things a little easier, to try to slow down the world somewhat. "That is a pretty good dream—a very big dream actually."

Ann has created balance in her life. She tries to keep time for herself as well as her affiliation with the Maine Olmsted Alliance for Parks and Landscapes and for her hobby of historic gardens. She loves to travel, particularly to the great gardens of Japan. On a daily basis she treats herself to a run, something she has done for twenty years. This also gives her some sense of quiet and is her spiritual time. She loves being outdoors. "That's when I'm most happy. That's when I sort out all the stuff that's going around in my head."

Ann's philosophy about life is, "Try lots of different things, different experiences, not only to find out what you like to do, but also to find those things that you don't really like ... You need to figure out how you like to spend your time. Is it outside or inside? Do you like to dress up, or live in jeans? Be comfortable. Be careful not to fall into the trap of thinking you want to make a lot of money, because money doesn't buy happiness. Travel, because that's broadening. Do something on your own and live on your own to find out about yourself, but always be true to yourself. Don't ever feel that you can't do whatever you want to do."

Augusta, Maine

Persistence in achieving her goals

RIVA BERLEANT

Castine, Maine   Born 1935
Cultural anthropologist and college professor

The 1930s, the period of the Great Depression in America, was an extremely difficult time for many. Unemployment hovered around 25 percent and wages were low. There was no safety net for the unemployed or the elderly until the latter part of the decade. Medical insurance was rare, afforded largely by the few who were still well off. Many thousands rode the rails, becoming roving vagabonds looking for work. Nature seemed to conspire to make matters worse. Droughts in the central plains caused enormous dust bowls where crops failed and cattle died. Many farmers gave up their land and became migrant workers, with a large percentage moving to California.

It was during this period that Riva Berleant was born. Her father had been out of work for a while. The family lived in Buffalo, New York, in a neighborhood of Poles, African Americans, and other Jews. Riva had no realization of the desperate situation in the country or in her own family; she knew only that something was terribly wrong at home, and learned later that part of the problem resulted from her father's gambling. As a result, she buried her nose in books from an early age; it was her way to escape. Riva's mother would drop her at the public library and Riva would read mythology, folklore, and books about children from many nations. Riva believes it was this combination—the mixed neighborhood, which she found rich and exciting, plus reading—that gave her an abiding interest in other cultures. It eventually led to her profession—cultural anthropology. Her interest was further affected by the family's move when Riva was nine years old. Although it was a step up, she describes the new neighborhood as "deadly dull, petite bourgeoisie ... I

131

thought my life had come to an end; it was like a living death." No longer did Riva and the other neighborhood children play in the streets. People in the "better neighborhood" remained inside their houses.

Riva's career path from school days in Buffalo to her eventual profession was circuitous and strewn with obstacles. Money was tight. Her father and mother opposed her choice of anything more ambitious than teaching grade school. Although Riva wanted to become an anthropologist, she was too insecure, had no clear sense of how to get there, and lacked role models to help point the way.

Her first step was attending what she terms a "streetcar university" in Buffalo. She could ride to school but live at home and hold a part-time job. The school did not offer anthropology, but it provided a basic liberal arts degree. To get around her father's refusal to sign a scholarship application, she applied for a New York State Regents scholarship given by examination. Because her father felt that four years of college was enough for her, she moved to New York City immediately after graduation so she could pursue her studies away from parental disapproval. She worked in the New York Public Library until she saved enough money to attend graduate school. Afraid to make the change all the way to anthropology, Riva worked toward a graduate degree in folklore. She says now, "Something happened to me that shrunk the spirit I had as a child on the streets in Buffalo. I think it happens to a lot of women. It made it hard for me to do what I really wanted." As a result, she dropped out of graduate school.

She married and had children. "But at a time when life is supposed to be rich with little children, it was poisoned by the thought I had not done what I wanted to do." Riva made a plan to earn money again so she could eventually fund her way to her goal. She entered the college where her husband was teaching and sought a degree as a librarian, something she could do while raising children. After graduating, she got a job as librarian in an archaeology museum. Two years later, with three children, she went back to graduate school and was able to get a graduate assistantship, which paid her way.

To complete the research and dissertation for her Ph.D., Riva had to write about a culture that had not been previously studied. She had to find a place that was healthy and safe enough to take her children. She discovered it on the small Caribbean island of Barbuda. She spent six months there with the children doing research, then a couple of months the following year to complete her research. The combination of this experience and finally getting her Ph.D. helped her overcome her earlier fears. "It was as if I had rebirthed myself, and the person I was meant to be finally emerged."

Riva quickly discovered, however, that there were no jobs for professors at the time. So she taught part-time, wrote articles, contributed to articles, continued her research, and in general worked to establish her reputation in the field. Six years later she landed a job at the University of Connecticut at the Torrington campus. She commuted weekends to Long Island, where her husband was teaching, and spent weekdays as a paying guest of a friend. In spite of the inconvenience, Riva had finally found satisfaction. As she says, "I was a good teacher, good researcher, good anthropologist, good writer, and I think that really made me more myself. I don't think there was anything else that would have made me as happy and satisfied."

Shortly before Riva got her teaching position, she applied for a postdoctoral fellowship with the Social Science Research Council. She was informed that she was an alternate; if someone who received the fellowship turned it down, she would get it. When Riva called the program officer for an explanation, she was told that the decision had been based on "imponderables." She asked, "Do you mean something like being forty years old instead of a recent graduate?" She was urged to reapply the next year (when she did receive the appointment). Riva tells the story to illustrate that she had finally found her voice, learned to stand up for herself instead of slinking into a corner and saying, "Well, they just didn't want me."

Even before Riva started teaching at the University of Connecticut (she taught there for twenty years), she and her husband, Arnold, spent summers in Maine. They started by renting houses; in 1995 they bought the house they now own. Arnold moved in immediately, but Riva was still teaching in Connecticut and spent vacations and long weekends in Maine until retiring in 1999. Since living here full-time, she has begun teaching some courses at the University of Maine at Orono. Meanwhile, she is writing and enjoying her garden.

Riva says she has always felt like an outsider. Perhaps it is because she is Jewish. Perhaps it's because she was taken from the mixed neighborhood where she felt at home to a more upscale situation where people didn't know their neighbors, and where she had to get to know a new group at school. In her teens, she found she wasn't interested in many of the things her peers were, so she read books. She says that her early tendency to escape from difficult situations allowed her to become "oblivious" to many things around her.

Riva describes herself as critical, analytical, clear-sighted, and contrary. In a quest unsupported by her parents and bereft of role models, these qualities have served her well. So has her single-minded persistence to achieve her goals.

Castine, Maine

*I cannot and will not
cut my conscience to
fit this year's fashions.*

— Lillian Hellman

A quiet force, secure in her own skin

MELISSA (MISSY) HATCH

Liberty, Maine   Born 1954
Yoga and macrobiotics teacher, mothers adults

Missy enters a room with a compelling aura of quiet strength and confidence. Although small and slight of build, she appears larger than life. She exudes so much open friendliness and caring that it is almost impossible not to like her immensely. When she talks, it is with that same quiet confidence and caring, all of which speaks volumes about how and where she was raised, the family that nurtured her, and her experiences ever since.

Missy is the last member of five generations of the Hatch family on Islesboro, and the youngest of three sisters. Her father was a carpenter and a caretaker for the property of summer folks. As Missy says, "You couldn't go anywhere on the island that you weren't known; you always knew everyone; and there was nowhere you couldn't go in complete safety." In the early years, Missy's mother taught school on the island. Later, when she began to develop symptoms of multiple sclerosis, she got a career counseling job at the University of Maine and came home weekends. This left most of the care in the hands of her father, who taught his three daughters everything he might have taught a son. There was no talk of anything that girls shouldn't try.

Partly because of her mother's focus on education, Missy attended Gould Academy in Bethel, then went to Springfield College in Massachusetts and received a degree in psychology. These were happy years, marred only by the death of her eldest sister in a car crash when her mother was driving—a tragedy that Missy says her mother never fully recovered from. Missy also joined one of the early Outward Bound groups on Hurricane Island, an experience that helped reinforce her

137

awareness of her own strength in the company of other strong individuals. She was appointed watch captain on her boat.

Before focusing on a career, Missy took a number of local jobs. She helped a friend build a house, spent two or three years teaching people to sail, worked in environmental education, and helped in her older sister's gardening business, where she especially enjoyed building rock walls, a skill that later became a form of therapy. She took the family catboat to The Bath Apprenticeshop and asked its director, Lance Lee, to let her undertake the boat's restoration. He later hired her. Thus began a ten-year association with the Apprenticeshop, at first in Bath but mostly after it moved to Rockport. She followed Lance around, cleaning up his offices as he moved from one to another. She worked on the organization's magazine, wrote news releases, developed exhibits and programs for the public—in general doing anything that came along. During this period she became close to a rigger and boatbuilder at the Apprenticeshop who would become her husband. After they married (she remained known as Hatch because she is the last to bear the name), they bought land in Liberty and started building a house, an ongoing process.

Around 1990, she began noticing blind spots in front of her eyes. A checkup revealed a slow-growing brain tumor. She resisted the recommendation for radiation treatments and opted instead for alternative methods—a decision she felt was very empowering and a first step toward self-healing. She took up yoga and meditation and learned about macrobiotic diets. She continued her attempt at self-healing for a year, then went back for another checkup. To everyone's surprise the tumor had disappeared.

The experience had a major impact on Missy. She studied macrobiotics at the Kushi Institute in western Massachusetts, and during summers she cooks for groups using macrobiotic methods. She pursues her study of yoga and teaches it in Belfast and Camden. She still builds rock walls for therapy, although less frequently than she did. She's mother to the adult community around her, someone whom people listen to. She is loved by many and is a quiet, positive force for everyone she knows. In her own words, "I like being strong. I feel strong—I like my lifestyle, what I'm doing. I feel it supports both me and the people I'm in contact with and is nurturing in sort of a non-traditional way. Vern and I decided not to have children, so I'm mothering adults and that suits me to a T."

Missy doesn't know what she'll do next. Her guiding principle is,

"To thine own self be true." Her dance with mortality made her add a second principle: "Just do it. Don't wait. What are you saving it for?" She is also aware of a third motivation: "Don't be so sure you know what should be happening."

Camden, Maine

Determined to do her own thing

SARAH (SALLY) HUDSON

Castine, Maine   Born 1947

Teaches ship's medicine, started local ambulance service

Sally's career decision made her the black sheep of an otherwise loving family. With a degree in economics, she turned down a high-paying position with the IRS to take a $1.50 per hour job in a doctor's office. She was one of four daughters of a successful Pittsburgh steel company owner who was looking to her to follow in his footsteps, and until then, she had been a dutiful daughter. This time, she put her foot down and said, "No. I need to do what I want to do." The decision made her feel lonely, but she remained in her job and started taking an EMT (emergency medical technician) course and otherwise furthering her medical education. She passed the X-ray technician exam, then became head of emergency room services at the tiny hospital in Castine. She started teaching ship's medicine at Maine Maritime Academy, also in Castine, began teaching EMT courses, and was named Maine EMT Instructor of the Year in 1990 and again in 1993. In addition, she started the Bagaduce Ambulance Service out of Castine and became a member of the governor's advisory board for emergency medical services.

The fact that the study of economics didn't much interest Sally was part of the reason she turned down the IRS job. She studied economics in the first place only because that's what her father wanted her to do. Her interest in medicine was probably first aroused by a favorite uncle who was a doctor. It probably helped that her family situation eliminated money as a primary motivation. Perhaps even more important was the influence of her grandmother—a world-class amateur golfer in the days when women didn't play golf—who impressed on Sally the idea that a girl could pretty much do anything she wanted to do. This idea was

141

reinforced strongly at Rosemary Hall, an all-girls' preparatory school she attended as a boarder. Here she learned that in order to do what she wanted, she had only to prove to the world that she could do it. The lesson convinced Sally of the value of single-sex education. Her achievements stand as a powerful testament to what passion can do. It should also serve as a warning to parents not to try to re-create themselves through their children.

Sally downplays another side of her story, largely because she chooses to live a relatively normal life despite having multiple sclerosis. She was first diagnosed with the disease as a sophomore at Colby College, going blind in one eye. The condition lasted only six months but made her miss a full semester's work, which she later made up in order to graduate with her class. Since then she has had three episodes of blindness, recovering each time. She has problems with one arm and has no feeling in one leg. So getting out of bed each morning and going places is part of what keeps Sally moving.

Beyond her grit, her accomplishments, and her strong belief in mind over matter, Sally's years of teaching have given her numerous opportunities to encourage young women to be all they can be. Her belief is that education is "empowerment"—whether or not it is in a person's field—that a woman can go through any educational process a man can, and in fact women are smarter than men in many educational settings. Sally points to the student chief engineer at Maine Maritime Academy: "Lindsey Smith is a young woman who can take apart the machinery on the academy ship faster than any of the men in her senior class."

Although Sally understands the pitfalls of having a career and rearing children at the same time, she believes that women need role models and the encouragement that comes from examples. They need someone saying, "Continue—you're doing a good job, although you might want to go on this track." Meanwhile she herself remains a strong role model. Her rewards come from former students calling from places as far away as the Indian Ocean saying, "I just saved a life" or "I just delivered a baby."

Castine, Maine

LIST OF PROFILES
By primary areas of involvement

Agricultural and fishing
   Swordfishing, lobstering—Linda Greenlaw
   Sheep farming—Nanney Kennedy
   Landscape contracting—Betty Ann Listowich

Art
   Poet, former poet laureate—Kate Barnes
   Musician, composer, teacher, bandleader—Mary Anne Driscoll
   Aerial and art photographer, singer—Rosalind Morgan
   Visual artist, landscape painter—Marguerite Robichaux

Business
   Web design for the Internet—Janet Harvie
   Excavation and road construction—Kathy Ouellette

Civil rights
   Writer of civil rights legislation, heads Maine LEAP—
      Kathryn McInnis-Misenor
   Coordinater of civil rights for Maine Department of Transportation—
      Penny Plourde

Independent, miscellaneous occupations
   Jill of many trades, lover of music—Muriel Curtis
   Long-distance trucker, diesel engine mechanic—Anneliese Francis

Nonprofit organizations
   Maine Women's Fund—Karin Anderson
   Atlantic Challenge Foundation—Cate Cronin
   Maine Island Trail Association—Karen Stimpson
   Center for Maine Contemporary Art—Sheila Tasker

Politics
   Newly elected state senator, sociol worker, psychotherapist—
      Lynn Bromley
   Elected chief of the Houlton Band of Maliseet Indians—
      Brenda Commander
   Representative of the Penobscot Nation in Augusta—Donna Loring
   Four-term state senator, running for U.S. senator—Chellie Pingree

Service professions

Law

    Attorney, women's advocate—Janet C. McCaa

Medicine

    Operating room and ICU nurse—Yueer (E R) Ren

    Forensic and clinical psychiatrist, writer—Diane H. Schetky

    Director of facility for the mentally ill, llama farmer—Joan Yeaton

Religion

    Ordained minister and parish pastor—Susan Stonestreet

    Universalist, religion student, sternman—Linda Thompson

Science

    Forestry and wildlife biology consultant—Linda Alverson

    Maine state horticulturist—Ann Gibbs

Teaching

    Professor of cultural anthropology—Riva Berleant

    Teaches yoga and macrobiotics—Melissa Hatch

    Teaches ship's medicine—Sarah Hudson